ELVIS McGONAGALL
VIVA LOCH LOMOND!
POEMS 2003-2017

Illustrated by Tony Kerins

Burning Eye

BurningEyeBooks
Never Knowingly
Mainstream

Copyright © 2017 Richard Smith www.elvismcgonagall.co.uk
Illustrations © 2017 Tony Kerins www.tonykerins.com
Cover photograph by Anna McCarthy www.annamccarthy.com

The author asserts the moral right under the Copyright, Designs and Patents Act 1988 to be identified as the author of this work.

All rights reserved. No part of this publication may be reproduced, stored in a retrieval system, or transmitted, in any form or by any means without the prior written consent of the author, nor be otherwise circulated in any form of binding or cover other than that in which it is published and without a similar condition being imposed on the subsequent purchaser.

This edition published by Burning Eye Books 2017

www.burningeye.co.uk

@burningeyebooks

Burning Eye Books
15 West Hill, Portishead, BS20 6LG

ISBN 978 1 90913 691 5

"Where Manchester has John Cooper Clarke, Dundee has Elvis McGonagall. Wonderful writing, tack-sharp humour and uncompromising politics. Hilarious."
(**** Marissa Burgess, The List)

"Bitingly satirical, irreverent, intelligent and laugh-out-loud funny, Elvis McGonagall has deservedly earned a reputation as one of UK performance poetry's most cherished stars."
(Nathan Filer)

"Funnier than most stand-ups, wittier than most wits, Elvis resides in zeitgeist, always passionately pushing the envelope. A class act."
 (Hardeep Singh Kohli)

"The poetry of Elvis McGonagall is a world steeped in the darkest humour, peaty whisky and joy and I love it – it is the profound humanity beneath the punchlines that melts my heart."
(Salena Godden)

"I couldn't imagine the poetry scene without Elvis McGonagall. His verse is wonderful – full of chippy invective and scorching satire. My favourite Elvis, just ahead of Costello."
(Luke Wright)

"Like a mini William Wallace of words giving the ruling political class the middle satirical finger Elvis puts the Bang into Bang Said The Gun every time he stands on our stage."
(Dan Cockrill & Martin Galton, Bang Said The Gun)

"A deep-fried ball of disillusioned bile stuffed into a tartan jacket and thrust on stage, Elvis McGonagall has us laughing through the tears as the ship sinks. Good hair, too."
(Jonny Fluffypunk)

"Ebullient, intelligent and deeply amusing sociopolitical satire."
(Murray Lachlan Young)

"Pin-pointed satires, dynamic performances and meticulous impressions. Electrifying, bitingly funny and politically astute."
(Michael Horovitz)

"McGonagalls? Deadbeat poet."
(Mr Szczypkowski, janitor and proprietor of the Promised Land Inconvenience Store at the Graceland Caravan Park)

"Someone you've never heard of whose every stanza sounds like it was written by Les Dawson on the back of a fag packet."
(Rachel Cooke, The New Statesman)

Stand-up poet, armchair revolutionary, comedian and broadcaster, Elvis McGonagall lives at the Graceland Caravan Park somewhere in the middle of nowhere where he scribbles verse whilst drinking Scotch, listening to Johnny Cash and throwing heavy objects at his portable telly.

Two series of his sitcom "Elvis McGonagall Takes A Look On The Bright Side" have been broadcast on BBC Radio 4 where he appears regularly as well as popping up occasionally on the television.

Elvis is the 2006 World Slam Champion*, the compere of the Blue Suede Sporran Club and performs at literary and music festivals, comedy clubs, pubs and dodgy dives up and down the country and abroad. The words in this volume are the sheet music for those performances.

*Scotland - world champions at curling, elephant polo and slam poetry. And, more recently, tennis.

In 2015 Elvis made the "Hot 100" – The List magazine's annual rundown of Scotland's "hottest cultural contributors". Possibly thanks to his jacket.

Deftly witty and subversive, Elvis has been spitting his scurrilous diatribes against the powers that be since 2003. And look at the state of the world now. So that's 14 years of futile ranting.

Elvis McGonagall has suffered for his poetry. Now it's your turn.

Tony Kerins has illustrated a barrowful of books but none with so many pictorial prompts to his imagination as this one. He's also painted over three hundred paperback covers, taught location drawing to art students and mapped illustrated walks for historic sites from Lands End to Stonehenge. For a period in the nineteen eighties, he was a contributor to Radio Times, providing celebrity portraits for the programmes of the day.

"Reality is so unspeakably sordid it make me shudder.*"
(Molesworth 2, 'Whizz for Atomms')

* The McGonagall family motto.

for Helen

CONTENTS

POLITICIANS 9

SCOTLAND 33

CELEBRITY 43

FOOD 57

THE COUNTRYSIDE 63

HAIKUS 73

BOOZE 77

EUROPE 81

WHIMSY 91

WAR 99

THE WEATHER 109

SMASH THE SYSTEM 115

ODDS AND SODS 133

POSITIVE POLLYANNA-ISH POEMS 139

GRAND ROYAL FINALE 143

I'M A BELIEVER

    Let me take you back to 2004 and the fag-end of Cool
    Britannia. Slap on Mr Tony's rictus Cheshire Cat grin, get
    out the glottal stops and work that mock Estuary English.

Let me simply say this to you
'Cos, hey look, y'know, I'm a pretty straight kinda guy
I only know what I believe
I believe in me, myself, I

I believe in forward not back, up not down
I believe I can fly
I believe I'm right, not left, in not out
I believe I can touch the sky

I believe children are our future
I believe in yesterday
I believe I didn't shout "Look! A big bad wolf of mass destruction!"
I believe a big boy did it and then he ran away

I believe in Christian soldiers marching onwards
I believe God told me to invade Iraq
I believe in the second coming of Jesus
Hallelujah! It's good to be back!

I believe going to war hurt me more than you
I believe my guitar gently wept
I believe history will judge me
I believe in Simon Schama – leather jacket, windswept

I believe George Bush is Gary Cooper
I believe I'm his Deputy Dog
I believe it's High Noon for Saddam Hussein
I believe Andrew Lloyd Webber looks like a frog

I believe the terrorists hate our way of life
I believe their bombs are much worse than ours
I believe Dr Evil and Mini-Me will be destroyed
I believe, yeah baby, I'm a little bit Austin Powers

I believe in the yellow brick road to Middle East peace
I believe the situation is sad, so sad, it's absurd
I believe Saturday night's alright for fighting
I believe sorry seems to be the hardest word

I believe in decent hard working families*
I believe we must change our pants and our socks
I believe in Newcastle Rovers
I believe opportunity knocks

I believe peace comes from the barrel of a gun
I believe liberty is a favourite shop of mine
I believe freedom is a song by George Michael
I believe truth is a perfume by Calvin Klein

I believe in privatised holidays in the sun
I believe in Silvio Berlusconi
I believe in a choice of luxury villas for everyone
I believe life is a minestrone

I believe I've got chums in America
From Milwaukee down to the Mojave
I believe in my special relationship
With a six-foot white rabbit called Harvey

I believe in a tall skinny decaff New Britain (don't I Harvey?)
I believe in my Emperor's New Burberry clothes
I believe in a flat-pack Britannia
I believe that for every drop of rain that falls a flower grows

I believe in Alastair Campbell's funky bagpipes
I believe in Melvyn Bragg's vibrant, bouffant hair
I believe in Rupert Murdoch
I believe in Rupert the Bear

I believe in Father Christmas
I believe in the Easter Bunny
I believe the tooth fairy is doing a jolly good job in difficult
    circumstances
I believe The Vicar of Dibley is really really funny

I believe that if you have a nasty bruise
"Ibuleve" will relieve it
But if someone says, "Hey, Tony! Y'know. Crikey! You could be
    wrong!"
Then I simply don't believe it

* "Hard working families" - the eternal joyless mantra of our politicians - what about drunken, feckless, childless, lazy poets eh? I've been disenfranchised.

BUSH TELEGRAPH

Time to mangle the Queen's English, Dubya style.

I'm Sheriff George Wayne Bobbitt Two
The Wild West's biggest dick
Saddam Insane's a captivated man
That guy was Hitleristic

He had an axe of evil
Though we're not sure where it's gone
His moustache of destruction
That weren't foolin' anyone

Them Muslin folk need civilized
Teriyakis must be free
They're dyin' for a Starbucks
'Cos that's democracy

I'm proud to be American
We gave the world french fries
Paris is in Texas
Jacques Garlic he tells lies

My cuddly buddy's Tony Bear
He lives in a clock called Ben
We play at Christian soldiers
Praise be for nukes, Amen

Your great Prime Mister Stan Church Hole
May I paraphrasicate?
"We fried eggs on their beaches
Over-easy, gas mark eight!"

We carpet bombed Beanbagdad!
Whizz bang biff bang pow!
Have a nice day Islaminates
It's Uncle Sam's oil now

THIS LAND'S NOT YOUR LAND

A Republican Party Protest Song - with apologies to Woody Guthrie.

This land's not your land, this land is our land
From Columbus Ohio, to the Florida swampland
From the corporate jungle to the redneck ranchland
This land was made by Fox TV

It's bible bashin' Disneyland
It's yippee-ai eye for an eye
It's faith, family and flag
God, guns and apple pie

This land belongs to cowboys
In Stetsons, spurs 'n suits
We're the Wall Street, Walmart Waltons
John-Boy, Jim-Bob, Jack-Boots

In the Burger Kingdom of The Stupid
Stupid is as Stupid does
Forrest Gump* is President
Yee-haw! He's one of us!

We're Starbuckin' bronco Marlboro' men
We're big chief swingin' dicks
It's John Wayne's world in Washington
We're the Capitol Hillbilly hicks

We don't read books, we do action
All-American wham bam ma'am!
Schwarzenegger Uber Alles!
Gimme five Jean-Claude Van Damme!

Rambo is not a poet
The French is arty-farty funks
We hate cheese surrender chimpanzees
We hate perverts, pansies, punks

'Cos them flip-flop pinko girly boys
They don't walk The American Way
The Dixie Chicks are Communists
SpongeBob SquarePants is gay

* Six-foot human glove puppet George W Bush. This 2005 poem was about the people with their hands up the puppet's arse. They almost seem sane now compared to the new President, Big Chief Yellow Hair or The Golden Toad as we like to call him round our way.

Hollywood is Satan's whorehouse
It's the Sodom 'n Gomorrah Motel
Route 666 to Tinseltown
Is the road to burnin' hell

We ride the hosanna highway
Saddle up our SUV
We got a two-ton tank 'n a ten-gallon hat
O-I-L spells victory

We're Team USA cheerleaders
Go! Go! Go! The Pentagon!
Shakin' 9/11 pompoms 24/7
Armageddon? Bring it on!

'Cos we're the evangelical vandals
Shit-kick, kick, kickin' down Mecca's door
Rainin' baptist bombs on Babylon
Behold their Shock 'n Awe!

We're pumpin' out Mohammed's diesel
Fillin' up Christ's limousine
Hallelujah Halliburton!
Glory! Glory! Gasoline!

Got no time for risin' oceans
Ozone layers or polar bears
Kyoto – is that a Japanese car?
It's gettin' hot in here – who cares?

We export Nike swoosh democracy
Handmade with Asian sweat
And golden arches of MacFreedom
Built on African debt

Charlie Darwin was a monkey boy
His science fiction's over
The Almighty made us, that's a fact
Way to go Jehovah!

The American Dream is born again
It's a big name brand New Deal
It's a holy roller Coca-Cola
Prozac Happy Meal

It's Britney Spears 'n Bud Lite beers
It's Super-Size 'n Super Bowl
It's Dunkin' Donuts on your mind
It's botox for your soul

We don't spare no cash for trailer trash
You gotta help yourself Jose
We wipe our ass with dollar bills
Da-doo Enron-ron have a nice day

We're the bullet-head neo-conmen
We're the mob that franchise fear
Cat Stevens is an evil terrorist
Folk with beards ain't welcome here

We zip 'em up like chocolate oranges
Shackle, cage, interrogate
We protect Wild West values
Strip, abuse, humiliate

We don't murder unborn babies
We're pro-life NRA
We Kentucky fry death row deadbeats
We're electric KKK

We're the Saxon sons of Uncle Sam
Our blood's red, white 'n blue
There ain't no black in the Stars 'n Stripes
It don't fly for Apache or Sioux

We have loosed the fateful lightning
Of our terrible swift sword
We're the Pentecostal patriots
Kick butt and Praise the Lord!

This land's not your land, this land is our land
From the buffalo Badlands to the cotton-pickin' Dixieland
From the Dust Bowl wasteland to the Presley Graceland
This land is Jesusland! Amen!

SON OF A PREACHER MAN

To be read in an uncomfortable, dour, Presbyterian voice, a wee bit constipated, a wee bit cucumber up arse.

This is my pledge to the British people
I will not let you down
I promise to do my utmost
I am Gordon, I am Brown

I will stand up for a serious Britain
I will stand up for minimum British fuss
I will stand up for sensible British values
I will stand up for old ladies on the bus

I will stand up for resolute British trousers
I will stand up for disciplined British queues
I will stand up for sturdy, stable British hair
I will stand up for tough, shiny British shoes

I will stand up for our new national anthem
"Heaven Knows We're Miserable Now"
I will stand up, stand up for Jesus
I will stand up for cheap underpants made in Guangzhou

I will stand up for neo-endogenous growth theory
Cross-collateralisation
Arctic Monkey inflation targets
Progressive rollover Raith Rover taxation

I will stand up for sober, British prudence
I will stand up to the global challenge of change
I will stand up for "Britain's Got Talent"
I will stand up with a smile that is honestly strange

In a drab, dreich, dreary monotone drone
Glaring, glowering, thundering cloud
Brooding, fuming, scowling, wuthering heights
Say it loud I'm Brown, I'm proud

Brown sauce, brown owl, brown sugar
Brown girl in the ring
Little brown jug, how now brown cow
Brown paper packages tied up with string

There'll be brown birds over the brown cliffs of Dover
Tie a brown ribbon round the old brown tree
It's good to touch the brown, brown grass of home
The lady in brown is dancing with me

Brown, brown, brown, brown, brown
Knees up Mother Brown
Mister Brown goes off to town
Brown, brown, brown, brown, brown

> Gordon Brown was actually christened "James Gordon Brown". If only he'd called himself James it could all have been so different!

The name's James Brown! McMotown Brown!
I feel good! So good it's sinister!
I'm the Walrus of Love, unnnh! A sex machine!
A super-bad-ass-motherfuckin' funky Prime Minister!

Eat yer heart oot Anorak Obama!
I'm the Scottish soul brother, I'm the daddy!
Papa's got a brand new bagpipe....unnnh! Hit me!
Get on the good foot laddie!

> What a tragic waste. I believe Gordon now plays Jazzer in The Archers.

YOU CAN CALL ME DAVE

Smooth, ever so smooth, modulated, round vowels. No hint of a glottal stop.

Change, Optimism, Hope
Progress, Energy, Vigour
Modest, Moderate, Modern
Brighter, Better, Bigger

Conservative, Compassionate, Liberal
Black, Muslim, Gay
Young, Green, Martian
Work, Rest, Play

Responsible, Tangible, Real
Motivation, Dedication, Aspiration
Empower, Enhance, Improve
Location, Location, Location

Freedom, Wealth, Opportunity
Courage, Resolve, Expertise
Beliefs, Values, Dreams
Eats, Shoots, Leaves

On, My, Bike
Eco, Friendly, Guy
Recycle, Renew, Relax
Take, Awf, Tie

Liberty, Equality, Paternity
Women, Babies, Men
Co-operation, Coalition, Cocaine?
Never, Ever, Again

Trusting, Caring, Sharing
Rebekah, Rupert, Andy
Emerson, Lake, Palmer
Yankee, Doodle, Dandy

Beanz, Meanz, Heinz
Ready, Steady, Go
Leg, Before, Wicket
Edgar, Allen, Poe

Mary, Mungo, Midge
Beverly, Hills, Cop
Yabba, Dabba, Doo
Snap, Crackle, Pop

Keep, It, Real
Watch, Me, Blog
Pimp, My, Ride
Snoop, Doggy, Dogg

Boo, Ya, Shaka
In, Da, Hood
Super, Smashing, Great
Finger, Lickin', Good

West, Ham, Villa
What, Ho, Jeeves
Bloody, Pumped, Up
Roll, Up, Sleeves

Suit, You, Sir
Are, Friends, Electric?
Want, That, One
Vorsprung, Durch, Technik

Bloody, Nice, Bloke
Sun, Shiney, Day
Blobby, Blobby, Blobby
Gabba, Gabba, Hey

Drivel, Piffle, Bilge
Yackety, Yack, Yack
Rhubarb, Rhubarb, Rhubarb
Quack, Quack, Quack

Silver, Spoon, Face
Chubby, Puppy, Fat
Shiny, Wavy, Hair
Notting, Hill, Twat

Same, Old, Tory
Eton, Blood, Blue
Brand, New, Package
Blair, Mark, Two

David Cameron. Not a shifty, oleaginous Mayfair estate agent apparently but an actual politician. Nay, a visionary statesman. He had plans but then so did Baldrick. It only took 10 years of performing this piece to get rid of him. That's the power of poetry.

53 QUID A WEEK

Here come's austerity's suffragette
With blue blood, toil, tears and sweat
It's Iain Duncan Antoinette*
On 53 quid a week

Dressed head to toe in condescension
Alarm-clock Britain's Mr Pension
Regrets? He'll have too few to mention
On 53 quid a week

Down the dole in his strawberry cords
Hanging out with the unwashed hordes
Yes all of us can live like Lords
On 53 quid a week

The hoi polloi are on the fiddle
Farewell welfare hey diddle diddle
Let them buy their cake at Lidl
On 53 quid a week

They all want more like Oliver Twist
Something for nothing – it's Trotskyist
Roman Abramovich could subsist
On 53 quid a week

Breadline Britain? Don't be facetious
The spongers are as rich as Croesus
Turn water into wine like Jesus
On 53 quid a week

Rent a council palace in Versailles
Feed your family pie in the sky
In cloud-cuckoo-land the pigs all fly
On 53 quid a week

Smith's out in the cold on easy street
Wrapped up warm in his self-conceit
"Does Aldi's sell Chateau Lafite?
One's on 53 quid a week"

Talk of poverty's tongue-in-cheek
The outlook's really not that bleak
It's "Nouveau Pauvre" – terribly chic
On 53 quid a week

Everybody's starving nowadays
And scurvy's such a common malaise
Hypothermia's the latest craze
On 53 quid a week

Drowning in debt? Then give us a wave
Sell yourself on eBay. Try to save
Dance as you dig your own pauper's grave
On 53 quid a week

* Nosferatu look-a-like and ex Work and Pensions Secretary Iain Duncan Smith told BBC Radio 4 that he could survive on £53 a week "if I had to". I wonder if he's seen "I, Daniel Blake"?

A BED AT THE RITZ

Empire's half-mast flag unfurls
Requiems tweet from ex-Spice Girls
Iron handbag, twin-set and pearls
Found dead in a bed at The Ritz

Cruel Britannia's buccaneer
Brass-balled female anti-Greer
Cause of Ben Bloody Elton's career
Found dead in a bed at The Ritz

Sybil-out-of-Fawlty-Towers-hair
Steel clad belief in laissez-faire
The midwife that gave birth to Blair
Now dead in a bed at The Ritz

Lovelorn acolytes sadly weep
Cue phony Tony so skin-deep
"Hey – she was the people's Meryl Streep"
Dead in a bed at The Ritz

Cold pre-packaged grocer's daughter
Leading England's lambs to slaughter
Ordained divine at Mammon's altar
Dead in a bed at The Ritz

Boudicca of entente cordiale
The Tory gentleman's femme fatale
Mandela's foe and Pinochet's pal
Dead in a bed at The Ritz

Fed the rich their daily focaccia*
Spawned men of Jeffrey Archer's stature
Besmirched the honest trade of thatcher
Dead in a bed at The Ritz

Here lies a shattered miner's lamp
Factories choked down in black damp
Belgrano ghosts still slowly stamp
Round and round a bed at The Ritz

You can pray Charon rows her to hell
"Tramp the dirt down", sound a futile knell
But all her dreams are alive and well
And living it up at The Ritz

Money shouts – just listen to the noise
Material Girls and City Boys
Ruthless Little Lord Fauntleroys
Even now they're putting on The Ritz

Public service sold for private wealth
Community and kindness killed by stealth
Compassion, care and national health
Dying in a sick-bed far from The Ritz

Put inequality to the sword
Give each one of us our just reward
And then one day we all might afford
To pay for a bed at The Ritz

* Somebody posted this poem on the internet and inserted a wee footnote like this, saying "I think the poet has used the word focaccia solely for the rhyme". Got me bang to rights son. Couldn't resist it. Focaccia is more of a New Labour bread really isn't it? A Peter Mandelson bread if you will. If such a thing exists and it probably does. Anyway, that's poetic licence mate. At certain venues this poem provokes audible gasps of horror followed by tumbleweed drifting through the room. Can't think why.

COLD COMFORT

The raven is croaking in the yew tree
The owl is shrieking in the withered oak
A dread leaden pall shrouds our barren land
Decay wraps us in his sulphurous cloak

The serpent slithers through the jungled weeds
The beast festers in its wormy bed
Fear is lurking in the sullen shadows
Deep in the cankered forest terror treads

The silver-mantled moon turns bloody
Dismal discord hammers in the forge
The jaws of darkness devour all hope
The wailing winter wind whispers "George"

Steeped in gore, caressed by Satan's claw
Out of Hades the devil's spawn is torn
I've seen something nasty in the woodshed
The Thing that dare not speak its name – "Osborne"*

Here's Georgie Porgie Prince of Darkness
Gnash your teeth, weep, rend your garments, writhe
Lock up your daughters he's the Poundland Poldark
A-wiggling his deficit scythe

Drop your trousers Britain, bend over
For the fiscal Wackford Squeers
A Reservoir Dogs' Mr Pasty Face
Busy chop, chop chopping off ears

"Not just a Chancellor, an S&M Chancellor"**
Marquis de Sade sour milk smile
Caligula in a Bob the Builder hat
Poverty's Mack the Knife, curt and vile

There's something nasty in the woodshed mother
Listen to my Edvard Munch silent scream
Oh sweet baby Jesus Christ almighty
Someone tell me that it's all a bad dream

* George Osborne - ex-Chancellor, millionaire and part-time Newspaper Editor, Investment Advisor, and Restoration Fop. Architect of Austerity Britain. Purveyor of his own brand of celebrity perfume - "Complacency" - for the man who doesn't have to try - at all.

** Sultry Marks & Spencer food voiceover voice here.

NARCISSUS IN BICYCLE CLIPS

Voice - Bertie Wooster silver spoon buffoon.

Cry hip hooray for Blighty
It's jolly voting weather
Squash the Frogs, send in the Clowns
What ho chaps altogether!

Straight outta Eton, MC Bojo
Little England's Mr Big
A six foot furry mascot
In an Andy Warhol wig

Walking, talking whoopee cushion
Rumpy-pumpy pants on fire
Porky pie man – what a whopper!
Dingle dangle on the old zip-wire*

* One of his carefully rehearsed spontaneous stunts.

Hokey-cokey referendum
In-out-up-down-back-to-front
Crikey! Shafted up the Brexit!
Et tu Gove? Cunning stunt!

Cripes and crumbs! Nil desperandum!
Boris bounces back – good golly!
Me, me, me – nunc est bibendum
May Day! May Day! Pass the Bolly

Johnny Foreign Secretary**
Bash the Boche and stun the Hun
Achtung Fritz! Clout the Kraut
Stick it up the Kaiser with a Gatling gun

What a tip-top-hat tofftastic time
Bunter's got the tuck shop keys
Respect the liquorice allsorts bro
Ooh-aah Cantonese

Get down with the ethnics
Yo! Word up Hippocrates!
Umbongo, Umbongo they drink it up the Congo
What a character, what a wheeze

Obama – "watermelon smile"
Hillary – "sadistic mental nurse"
Hi-de-Heil Angela Hitler
Drivel, piffle – yikes! – next verse

Whiff-whaff-bat twat diplomat
Big white chief meet piccaninny
"That Ankara wankerer rogers goats"
"Everyone's a cannibal in Papua New Guinea"

Blah-blah Brussels, blah-blah-bollocks
Mumble, bumble, what a bore
Can I stop playing games now Matron?
This joke isn't funny anymore

** Boris Johnson - perfidious Albion's court jester. The day he was appointed Foreign Secretary may have been the day that satire died. Mr Johnson (let's get rid of the whole chummy "Boris" thing) was once quizzed about his £275,000 a year Daily Telegraph column. "Chickenfeed" he responded. That's a **bloody big** chicken he's got there.

AN APOLOGY

I promised not to break my promise
Broken promises were in the past
I vowed I'd write a poem about Nick Clegg*
But I'm sorry – I couldn't be arsed

* A man with the demeanour of a sad-eyed spaniel glumly fetching his master's slippers, aka the miserable ferret of compromise running up England's coalition trouser-leg for five long years.

FLIGHT OF FANCY

Oh would that I could fly unto the heavens
To clutch the universe in outstretched hand
To hover over stars like bees to flowers
To see the world as a tiny grain of sand

To drift like thistledown around the moon
The vaulted firmament my canopied bed
Oh for the wings, the wings of a pigeon
So I could shit on top of Donald Trump's head

Like Abba, I have a dream - except I believe in Engels.

You gotta have a dream to have a dream come true. This is mine. "God Save The Queen" being replaced by "Remember You're A Womble" - that's another one.

It's easy to make fun of whatever it is that's on Trump's head. So let's do it…

31 DESCRIPTIONS OF DONALD J TRUMP'S HAIRCUT

Acrylic ginger gerbil comb over
Guinea pig wig from Peru
Arthur Scargill joke shop syrup
A merkin for a kangaroo
Chain-smoking badger's nicotine stained coiffure
A shag-pile sample from "Carpet Right" – "apricot blush"
A Flock Of Seagulls tribute act *
A fascist furball coughed up by a giant ginger tom cat that looks like Hitler
"Bouffant Baboon" by Vidal Sassoon
A wee furry boudoir where Mick Hucknall sleeps at the weekend
A Liberace quiff sculpted from a jar of Cheez Whiz
Unidentifiable roadkill resting in peace
Jason and the Argonauts' Golden Fleece
A rampaging mandril's angry mullet
A Turner Prize winning art installation made by Edward Scissorhands from fibreglass insulation, snake oil, half a Weetabix and some bits found at the bottom of a budgie's cage
Something a squirrel has just shat on his heid
An old exhausted bri-nylon hamster dunked in a bowl of chicken-tikka-masala
A prop from the set of the musical "Strawheided Donald"
Manhattan-Muppet-Mussolini mop-top
The bastard offspring of a randy raccoon and Piers Morgan
24 karat gold candyfloss spun from the gossamer thin threads of a philistine's soul
Diabolical follicled flaccid ferret
The tangerine crème filling found in Forrest Gump's box of chocolates carelessly smeared all over his noggin
Runner up in a Gordon Strachan look-a-like contest at the Bonnie Prince Charlie Karaoke 'n Cocktail Lounge in Brooklyn
Polyester poodle parlour polecat pompadour
A style that would look good under a pointy white hood
Chewbacca's armpit velcroed to his bonce

The Reims Cathedral of tonsorial art for the man whose name
  means fart
Narcissistic, misogynist, mendacious, racist, reckless, rancorous,
  ugly, selfish, smug, sclerotic, subliterate, incoherent, ignorant,
  venal, vain, vindictive, arrogant, loathsome, fearmongering,
  hateful, bloviating, bombastic, bilious, berserk, pusillanimous,
  puerile, petulant, paranoid shampoo and set
Beelzebub's bully boy blow-wave
The Devil's Haircut

* He must be a Flock of Seagulls fan. Probably dances round his Louis XIV bedchamber in nothing but a pair of gold lamé chuddies** to "I Ran (So Far Away)" thinking the song is a handy guide to the geography of the Middle East. Incidentally, the band's lead singer was an ex-hairdresser.

** Chuddies are the Hinglish*** word for underpants. And this is a footnote to a footnote.

*** Hinglish is a hybrid of English and south Asian languages. And this is a footnote to a footnote to a footnote. Like those wee matryoshka dolls.****

****Matryoshka dolls are sets of wooden Russian dolls of decreasing size placed one inside another. Like this footnote to a footnote to a footnote to a footnote.*****

***** That's quite enough footnotes for this page.

SCOTLAND

THE WRONG SPORRAN

The Ballad 'O William Wallace & Gromit*

After a hard day's "FREEDOM!" fighting
Bringing the English to their knees
Ah pop oan ma tartan slippers
And eat a nice piece 'o Wensleydale cheese

*176 and a half minutes shorter than Mel Gibson's "Braveheart" and all the better for it I feel. Try reading this in Mr Gibson's "Scottish" accent for a laugh.

NICE TO SEE YOU TO SEE YOU NICE

The Ballad 'O Robert The Bruce Forsyth

In 1314 at Bannockburn
Proud Edward's army fell
The Scots won the battle and a cuddly toy
Oh didn't they do well? *

* That's Scottish history dealt with.

BIBLE BASHING

Knock, knock.

"Who's there?" we asked.
A reasonable question at such an unreasonably early hour on a wet Sunday morning in the fair city of Perth.

"Jehovah's Witnesses" replied the taller of the two short-back-and-sides-sober-suited-shiny-shoed gentlemen shuffling on our doorstep.

"Jehovah's Witnesses who?" we said peering round our father's legs as he stood akimbo on the Welcome mat.

"Jehovah's Witnesses who are waiting for The Second Coming, The Divine Purification and Imminent Armageddon" said the tall one waving a copy of The Watchtower in the air.

"We've just come for a brief chat" he added.

"Very brief" said my father as he slammed the door in their face.*

* A true story. My Dad didn't care for unexpected visitors. Particularly door-to-door God salesmen.

TRAINSPOTTING: A RAILWAY STORY

by The Very Reverend Irvine Welsh

Warning: Scottish vernacular employed in this poem.

Thomas The Tanked-Up Engine
Wis playin' wi' his Mainline Friends
He wis puffin' like a shite auld choo-choo
He couldnae chuff-chuff roond the bends

So Big Jimmy the fuckin' Red Engine
Rolled up 'n gie Tam a wee smoke
"Can I interest ye in some refreshments?" he said
" 'Cos things go better wi' coke"

Wouldn't it be brilliant if Irvine Welsh wrote children's books?

"Ye can keep yer toasted sangwidges 'n snacks
And yer individual fruit pies
Ma buffet car's sorted fer e's 'n wizz
Help yersel tae the goods – privatise!"

"Toot! Toot! This fare's just the ticket!"
Whistled Tam as he shot up the track
"Let's take a trip through the tunnel o' love
A have it away day oan smack!"

Whoo-whoo! What a rush! Tam wiz speedin'!
"Hullo! Railway Children! Let's rave!"
Jenny Agutter's whipped oaf her knickers
Tae gie Tam a special wee wave

"Look at me! Ah'm The Flyin' Fuckin' Scotsman!" said Tam
"Ah go jet set tae Rio – first class!
Je suis un Eurostar train trash
Adios Airdrie ya bass!"

The Fat Controller wiz ootay his box
The radge wiz goin' loco
"Yer the 2.33 tae Cowdenbeath
No Acafuckinpulco!"

"This is Virgin on the ridiculous!" said the boss
Then the buffer gie Tam the big shunt
"Yer scrap son – git oan the heave-ho express"
Tam laughed, "Fuck oaf ya fat cunt-roller"*

* Cheap laugh available here by leaving a wee pause halfway through pronouncing controller.

36

Bing! Bong! Tannoy announcer - nasal

"We interrupt this poem tae make a customer service announcement
Fer youse wankers oan platform eight
We're sorry fer the delay but the trains are oan drugs
That's why they're aw fuckin' late"

NORTH OF THE BORDER

Warning: more Scottish vernacular.

We were on the rampage doon frae Ecclefechan
Maraudin' o'er the Whin Sill tae Bardon Mill village
We were gonnae rustle cattle, snaffle chattels, have a battle
We were up fer a wee bit 'o pillage

But when we charged across the crags, lungs burstin'
Oor war cry slowly wheezed like a bagpipe's dying fall
We dropped oor claymores, we stood stock still
Some radge called Hadrian had built a fuckin' wall!

Fifteen foot high, ten foot thick
Seventy mile wide
How were we gonnae get a curry frae Vindalooland?
The takeaway was on the other side

This bampot Hadrian had an "Empire" frae Newcastle tae the Nile
But he didnae want oor wee bit hill an' glen
It's "civilisation fer the nation" – except fer us
Everybody's pickin' on the Picts – again

So Big Murdo McBanksy drew his sgian-dubh and scribbled
    in the stone –
"Redire ad Romanum Magnum Nasus"
Which means – "Fuck off back tae Rome ya big nosed bastard"
Aye – we're no so "barbarian" as some o' youse paints us

We didnae sail doon the Dee on a digestive
We can haud oor heids high like thistles, we're fine
Youse can keep yer libraries, yer baths and yer togas
Yer latrines, yer sandals and yer wine

Stick yer aqueducts where the sun don't shine
And every endless, boring, boring road
We will not be subjected to yer oppressive, supremacist, cultural
    imperialism pal
Because....err....we just like wearing woad

And because we come frae bonny Caledonia
Land o' the mythical useless goalie
Deep-fried Mars bars, North Sea oil
Sean Connery 'n Hardeep Singh Kohli

Kippers, kilts 'n the Krankies
Haggis, Highland fling 'n Hogmanay
Tartan, tarmacadam, television
And the beautiful silvery Tay

Sporrans, porridge, penicillin, Rabbie Burns
Rab C Nesbitt, Andy Murray, Auld Lang Syne
Bay City Rollers, chronic heart disease
Lochs full o' whisky, we're a liquid goldmine

Which is why one day we came tae realise
Yon Hadrian was a right clever yin
This wall wasnae built tae keep us oot
It was built tae keep the English in

And though it has now fallen intae ruin
Like a phoenix frae the ashes it will rise up again
Because Scotland's gonnae rebuild the whole bloody thing –
Now that wee numpty Cameron's got intae Number Ten*

* He's gone now but so's our EU membership so who knows what's next?

Written for 2010's "All Along The Wall" project.

THE SCOTTISH LION'S RAMPANT

Yet more Scottish vernacular but there's a glossary over the page.

Come all youse glaikit farts in a trance
Grasp the thistle – let's go freelance
Do the Tunnock's Teacake dance
The Scottish Lion's rampant!

Get yersel' tae the faintheart surgeon
Leap like a Salmond, float like a Sturgeon*
Let the flower 'o Scotland burgeon
The Scottish Lion's rampant!

* Great line even if I say so myself. You write a line like that you do a wee dance and take the rest of the day off, go for a pint.

Gie it laldy pal, c'mon big yin
Dinnae shilly-shally, that's a sin
Open up Pandora's shortbread tin
The Scottish Lion's rampant!

Ignore the media mafiosi
Wee Fat Eck's no Keyser Soze
The future's fandabidozi
The Scottish Lion has roared – grrr!

Let's go Nordic – what a braw idea
Build an egalitarian state right here
A flat-pack Scandi "Och Aye-Kea"
Den Skotska Lejonet ar valdsam!

It's a modern modus operandi
Read the constitution in "The Dandy"
We'll aw get subsidised houghmagandie
The Scottish Lion's gone for his messages

Fair square sausage, better buttery rolls
Free tartan baffies for poor auld souls
World Cup finals full o' Scottish goals
The Scottish Lion's iron like a lion in Zion

We drink oor voddy wi' Irn-Bru
Oor pandas eat deep-fried bamboo
We'll swap yon Trident fur a sgian-dubh
In the jungle the mighty jungle the Scottish
    Lion's sleeping off a wee hangover tonight

Mais oui – nous sommes ecossaise
We're European pal – no petit anglaise
We'll dunk oor chips in mayonnaise
Viva Il Leone Scozzese!

Oh I would walk five hundred miles
For one 'o Jocky Wilson's smiles
Wee men in anoraks – that's oor style
The Scottish Lion's wearing a ginger jimmy bunnet

Land fit for aw us glorious losers
Land o' cholesterol and jam packed boozers
Let's aw sing "Donald Trump Where's Yer Troosers?"
The Scottish Lion's dancing a Dashing White Sergeant

Release the monster frae outta Loch Ness
Enough o' aw this Brexit mess
Stand up Scotland – next time – yes!
The Scottish Lion's rampant!
Go on – gie him a cuddle
He doesnae bite – much

This poem started life as "Stop Yer Swithering Jock" and was written for Bang Said The Gun's "Page Match" at the Edinburgh Book Festival in 2014. It was aimed at undecided voters in the independence referendum who were confused by Westminster politicians' sudden declarations of love - "Don't go Scotchland! We love you, we love you, you little drunken, ginger curiosities you".

It metamorphosed into this form in the wake of the 2015 SNP landslide and Alex Salmond's assertion that "the Scottish lion has roared".

"The Scottish lion" is a creature I was hitherto unaware of. Should be lioness really. Because the lion, like the male of most species, is a lazy arse. The women do all the work. The lion just sits around all day wondering what's for his tea and tossing his mane of hair like Neil Oliver off of "Coast" on a windy day. So this is dedicated to a Scottish lioness, Mhairi Black MP.

GLOSSARY

"glaikit fart in a trance" = a vacant person who seems disconnected from reality

"Tunnock's Teacake" = a sweet Scottish delicacy, giant versions of which featured in a dance at Glasgow's Commonwealth Games opening ceremony in 2014

"gie' it laldy" = do it with great gusto

"fandabidozi" = great, smashing, super as popularised by Wee Jimmy Krankie

"Den Skotska Lejonet ar valdsam!" = the Scottish Lion's rampant! I knew watching The Bridge, The Killing and The Wallander would come in handy one day. Although even if you like the Nordic Noir you must admit it's just Taggart with expensive jumpers really

"houghmagandie" = fornication

"go the messages" = to shop for everyday goods such as foodstuffs

"square sausage" = a traditional Scottish breakfast food

"buttery" = a savoury, Scottish bread roll

"baffies" = slippers, preferably ankle-length with a zip up the front

"Irn-Bru" = a Scottish carbonated soft drink, similar in colour to Donald Trump's visage

"sgian-dubh" = small knife stuffed down the sock of a kilt-wearing gentleman

"Viva Il Leone Scozzese!" = Long Live the Scottish Lion! I knew watching Inspector Montalbano would come in handy one day

Jocky Wilson = late, great darts champion who didn't look after his teeth

"Jimmy bunnet" = tartan joke shop hat with ginger wig attached

"Dashing White Sergeant" = a Scottish country dance performed in groups of six people

THIS MUCH I KNOW

Don't know much about Einstein's theories
Don't know much about Newton's laws
Don't know much about Archimedes' principles
Or Mendel's megaspores

Don't know much about Hubble's telescope
Don't know much about Fermat's theorem
Don't know much about Foucault's pendulum
Or Edward Jenner's serum

Don't know much about Schrodinger's equation
Or Nobel's TNT
Don't know much about Euclid's elements
It's all bloody Greek to me

But here's a scientific fact any fool knows
Even if you're bottom of the class
It's a universal truth and it simply states –
Jeremy Clarkson is an arse!

Jeremy's hair is Shredded Wheat
His brains are Heinz Baked Beans
Jeremy likes to squeeze himself
Into very, very, very tight jeans

He's a 1970's throwback
He's Reactionary Man
He loves women – in bikinis on the bonnet of a Porsche
He's the flag in Little England's white van

Jeremy laughs at Johnny Foreigner
He's thinks left-wing polar bears are gay
He hates eco-mentalist vegan cyclists
He's a testosterone cliché

Jeremy blows up caravans!
Jeremy plays with big boys' toys!
Jeremy loves a phallic Ferrari
Speed, power, death and engine noise!

He's all Turbo-Diesel-Bitch-on-Heat
Twin-Lesbo-Gear-Box Blah Blah Blah
Don't wet your pants Jeremy
It's only a fucking car

But Jeremy adores 4 by 4's
He thinks anyone who doesn't is strange
He loves to burn up fossil fuel
He's got no time for climate change

Because Jeremy's far too busy
Jeremy likes to party
Pop another cork and snigger at the
Weardie-beardie arty-farty

'Cos global warming's mumbo-jumbo
When you're an egomaniac
Who cares about Bongo Bongo land?
Jeremy's all right Jack

So when the ice-caps have all melted
When the forests are aflame
When London drowns like Venice
Then we'll all know who to blame

Oh Jeremy deserves so much more
Than a custard pie in the face
Let's build a rocket out of Chelsea tractors
And blast him into space

With a one way ticket to a big black hole
As the petrol pumps run dry
It's the motormouth muppet's curtain call
Mr.Gobby is waving goodbye

Yes Jeremy Clarkson was an arse
Let's set that epitaph in granite
And when there's no more Jeremy Clarksons
Then we might just save this planet

> Of course he isn't just a 100 percent evil pub bore who talks in italics. He once punched Piers Morgan in the face. Well done Jeremy. But then came Steak-gate. So still an arse then.
>
> To be fair it's not just Clarkson causing global warming. It's cows farting as well. Yes bovine flatulence will help end the whole human vanity project. Which is strangely comforting. And then the planet will just lay fallow for a few million, million years. So nothing to worry about.

THE INEXORABLE MARCH OF WESTERN CULTURAL HEGEMONY*

The unorthodox priest in the wraparound shades
and the black gothic garb of his creed
Sits and flicks his worries away
bead by bead by bead
To the syncopated beat of the backgammon board
at whitewashed "Taverna Niko"
Where the traveller drinks in the afternoon sun
in a woozy Ouzo glow

As the inky blue turquoise Aegean
caresses the pink of the sand
While the sweet smell of thyme drifts by on a breeze
blessed balm for the heat of the land
Whose orchards hang heavy with lemons and figs
and the poppies dance under the trees
Where the olive groves groan with the honey-drip drone
of a thousand drowsy bees

And I think that I may have found paradise
bewitched by Persephone's kiss
A gift from Greek gods, heaven on earth
a moment of rapturous bliss
When a cry ricochets round the harbour
from the stereo on Stelios' boat
It's a sound that could shatter the crockery
like the bleat of a hideous goat:

"You're beautiful, you're b******ul
You're b******ul it's t***
I saw your **** in a crowded *****
And I don't know what to **
'Cos I'll never ** with ***"

> These should be the lyrics of an inexplicably popular weedy love song which can't be quoted here because it's copyright material and much too expensive to reproduce in full. The singer basically asserts that the object of his unrequited desire is rather good looking. Three times he says this. It's true.

And I realise God is a bastard
his divine holy love is a front
For no God of compassion or mercy
would have given us James Fucking Blunt**

* This poem should really be called "Paradise Lost" but some other bastard's already nicked that title. Anyway, never go back to somewhere you once had an idyllic holiday - you'll only be crushingly disappointed.

** James Blunt has had a ski lift named after him in Verbier. He's said that he's installing a sound system on it that will only play his music "to keep the queues down". Nice self-deprecation there James. Good work. I still hate that song though. And skiing.

JUSTICE

Sing hosanna! Sound the trumpet!
Kill the fatted calf!
Put out the bunting! Clash the cymbals!
Drink and dance and laugh!

Pay no heed to global warming
Bird flu, terrorists, Iraq
Yippee-ai-ay! It's A Beautiful Day –
Bono's got his Stetson back!

It's a broad-brimmed holy relic
"Symbolic" and "iconic"
High-crowned sartorial statement
"Authentic" and "ironic"

With no broncobuster's bonnet
Bono was monochrome
A bare-headed, stack-heeled leprauchaun
Lost in rock's enormo-dome

'Cos you can't sing stadium anthems
Full of righteous sound and fury
When your stylist's nicked your cowboy hat
And you look like Nana Mouskouri

It's worth every single million euros
Paid in U2's lawyers' fees
It's worth days and weeks and months in court
To help poor wee billionaire grandees

For now poverty will be history
There will be peace on earth
The lamb will lie down with the lion
There'll be joy and a new virgin birth

It's salvation for our planet
We're all winners, none of us losers
'Cos he also got back two souvenir mugs
And his pair of leather troosers

They're his troosers of philanthropy
His troosers of compassion
And if you're going to save a continent in crisis
You gotta feel good about fashion

You can't just wear a wristband
You need Red Armani shades
You need conspicuous consumption
Charity begins in shopping arcades

But now every little thing's gonna be alright
Bono's found what he was suing for
Rejoice on the plains of Africa!
There'll be a harvest for the world and more

There'll be rivers made out of chocolate
There'll be mountains of ice-cream
There'll be rainbows and skipping and puppy dogs
Love will reign supreme

So whoop and yell, hip, hip hooray!
Crack open the champagne
Hallelujah brothers and sisters!
It's the end of all sorrow and pain

Now his halo shines so bright tonight
Round his special, magic hat
Yes Bono's got his Stetson back
The sanctimonious twat

In 2006 Bono successfully sued U2's former stylist for the return of a Stetson hat and other items. A proud day for the Irish legal system. Aren't tax avoiding rock star philanthropists great?

THE END IS NIGH

Sponsored by the Daily Mail

We're doomed, we're damned, we're sitting ducks
We're stuffed, we've cooked our goose
The ravens have fled the tower
The chickens have come home to roost

We're sick as a parrot, we've had it
There's nothing we can cock-a-doodle-do
Just watch the bootiful birdies sneeze
Here comes the avian flu

On the wings of Hungarian turkeys
Asylum seeking foreign fowl
The feathery friends of grim-visag'd death
(Who looks like Simon Cowell)

Yes holy terror's in the air
The Sword of Damocles hangs overhead
Be afraid, be very afraid
The Taliban are under the bed

They've got hairy, scary, big, bad beards
They've got packages that are suspicious
There's bombs in those rucksacks 'n Reeboks
Tonight we'll all sleep with the fishes

As Dr.Evil cries "Havoc!
Let loose the dogs of nuclear war!"
Pointing his weapons at Mr Bean's Britain –
Blighted Blighty will soon be no more

Thanks to that man who's running Iran
And the funny wee bloke from Korea
Tescos will tumble, house prices will crash
Gotterdammerung is here!

"Up there!" Shouts Lembit Opik
"Asteroids falling from the sky!"
And both the Cheeky Girls agree
Oh no! We're all gonnae die!

As the oceans boil and the icebergs melt
And the scorched earth burns in the sun
Emperor Nero is playing his fiddle
Pandemonium's reign has begun

And the molten rivers are rising
Fire 'n brimstone floods the land
We're down the final furlong
The Day of Judgment is at hand

It's the coup de gras, the KO blow
The last trump's blast, the death knell ring –
The Four Horsemen of the Apocalypse
War, Famine, Pestilence – and Sting

Yes – the King of Pain and pomposity
Eco-warrior-bringer-of-peace
Jaguar-car-flogging-rainforest-saviour
Chief Constable of The Police

The three-headed peroxide monster
That guards the gates to Hades
Beelzebub's troubadours trousering cash
As they yodel "Roxanne" for the ladies

Oh why Lord why must Sting still sing?
Lord when will he be mute?
Why can't he stick to tantric sex
And plucking his fucking lute?

I'll send an SOS to the world
With a desperate gasping breath
Here's my message in a bottle
O Sting, where is thy death? *

It's the planet's showstopping finale
Man's last words at the dying of the light
"De Do Do Do. De Da Da Da"
The End. I thank you. Goodnight

> * Sometimes you have to write an entire poem because you've got one line you really like. This pile of overwritten apocalyptic drivel was a result of "O Sting, where is thy death?" He's still with us (or was at the time of publication at least).

DE PROFUNDIS CLAMAVI AD TE, DOMINE (OUT OF THE DEPTHS HAVE I CRIED UNTO THEE, OH LORD) BY DAVID BECKHAM

For best results this should be read in a half-strangled, pinched bollock Essex falsetto.

I have suffered the slings and arrows of outrageous fortune
To perfidious fate I am in thrall
Now once more I must imbibe from the bitter cup of pain
Mine is the misery, the wormwood and the gall

My soul is bound upon a wheel of fire
My tears burn like molten lead
I am sunk in the wretched Slough of Despond
Thorns and nails my bed

Torment is heaped upon torment
All is turmoil, Sturm und Drang
The angels weep, proud Albion falls silent –
Alas – me Achilles tendon's gone twang

And so I sit with foot kaput upon the bench of angst
Hors de combat in my Sunday suit
As English hearts of oak are broken by German wunderkind
Our dreams of glory crushed under das jackboot

Tragedy clothed in sceptred pall
Sweeps over me as in Othello
For now I have been told that I am too old
By the evil Mister Capello

Yet this burden of grief is too, too much
For my heavy heart to carry
Jules Rimet's holy grail is forever out of reach
I feel like Tantalus in Hades, Gary

Tattooed of torso, perfumed of beard
Downcast I stare from yesterday's billboards of fame
The golden balls that launched a thousand pairs of pants
Will nevermore bejewel the beautiful game

Oh soothe my fevered brow Victoria
Sing me lullabies from when you was Posh
For all I can hear now is Edvard Munch's "Scream"
My mind is a painting by Hieronymus Bosch

No more will I charge unto the breach as three lions roar
No more will I bend the ball like – me
All my hopes in endless ruin lie
A man of sorrows, oh Lord I cry to thee

I am woebegone, oh woe, thrice woe
I know not how to express my distress
The despair, the dismay, the Weltschmerz
The agony, the anguish, the tristesse

Thus clutching at shadows I pen this my requiem
A wounded warrior in his lonely LA garret
And at the end of the day, to be fair, like I say
I'm as sick as a fucking parrot

> Young David is a successful graduate of the Elvis McGonagall Poetry Correspondence Course. The only one to date to be honest. This moving piece deals with his 2010 World Cup disappointment and I feel is one of his best efforts although he's let himself down with that last line - a wee bit tawdry.

RHYME-AID

How long must we hear their suffering?
Their senseless pain is a mystery
Let's hold hands, let's wear wristbands
Let's make Coldplay history

Sometimes you just have to make a stand against injustice and cruelty.

DESIGNER PORRIDGE

Apricot boilersuit by Versace
Diamante handcuffed glamour
We're winning the War on Celebrity
Paris Hilton is back in the slammer

FIFTY SHADES OF GRAYSON PERRY

Oh what a shock
Is it art or is it crockery?
He might wear a frock
It's Essex trannie pottery

He paints kids on his pots
But it ain't Harry Pottery
And it ain't exactly
Very terracottary

His pots cost a lot
Since he hit the jackpottery
I saw him on the telly
When he won The Turner lottery

He looks better in a dress
Than Rodney Trotter-y did in those crap ads
    for WH Smith
If you order Tarka Dhal
It's mainly ottery

His best friend's a bear
Called Alan Measles
Which doesn't rhyme with potter's wheel –
Sadly – only easels

So I went to The Tate
To have a look and whatnottery
And I loved Perry's pots
It's not tosspottery

Grayson Perry – respect urned

FOOD

JAMIE OLIVER TWIST

By Chas 'n Dave Dickens

Oi! Mr Bumble! I want more!
I'm gagging for it, know what I mean?
None of them turkey twizzlers guv!
I want the posh nosh tosh cuisine!

So bish bosh bash let's 'av some truffle mash
Wiv the old hot sausage 'n mustard
An ow's abaht a mascarpone tart?
Whack it in like wiv the old custard

Well oom-pah-pah I'm the nuddy chef
I'm choppin' up me chillies on the telly
Wicked. Love it. Superb and all that
Pan-fried eels in jelly!

'Oo will buy my Jack the Lad cookbooks?
You little tiger. Happy days!
Dahn The Isle of Thanet wiv a pomegranate
Cheeky chappy chops lyonnaise

Oozy wet polenta up the Jobcentre
Shout goin' out for charidee
Fifteen sprogs in a kitchen. Sweet
Bloomin' gorgeous. MBE!

Luvverly jubberly bubbly beans
Best baked bean bruschetta
Seven quid for beans on toast
Beanz meanz a new Lambretta!

Blinky, blonky, blimey, doolally stylee
Pearly King prawn – 'av a scallop
Pork pie 'n liquor vicar, awright John
Get minted – flash, bang wallop!

Oi Mr Sainsbury! I want more ads!
I'll do anyfing for you me old mucker
We gotta pick a pocket or two my son
Is that annuver cheque? Well pukka!

> Jamie's not the worst. Heston Blumenthal's the really annoying one. He doesn't even exist. That's Wayne Rooney in a pair of giant lab specs.
>
> This poem was written in 2004 when Jamie Oliver's ubiquity was starting to grate and celebrity chefs were suddenly everywhere.
>
> "Seared carpaccio of Aberdeen Angus with vermicelli broth served in an envelope of plastic" anyone? No, that's a beef pot noodle.
>
> "Haricots napolitanas on char-grilled ciabatta with chilli and Parmesan"? Cheesy beans.
>
> Next week Hugh Fearnley-Whittingstall in "Riverdance Cottage". Ethical cooking - no hands!

THE LORD AND MASTERCHEF*

He fed five thousand followers
With Hovis and some haddock
He turned Perrier to Pinot Noir
Eat yer heart oot Fanny Craddock

*Jesus - the first celebrity chef

GOODBYE GASTRONAUT

Unstop all the corks, shuck oysters by the dozen
Cook a coq au vin with gusto unalloyed
Have a quick slurp of Chateau Joie de Vivre
Then have another for Keith Floyd*

*proper chef

EATING OUT

Don't want food "plated up" by Jackson Pollock*
Don't want spuds sculpted like mini Taj Mahals
Don't need a night sky of Michelin stars
Don't need a right load of old Blumenthals

Just give me a taverna on an island
Ouzo and pistachios for starters
Plump purple oily olives, hunks of bread
Dunked in pale white taramasalata

An Aegean breeze full of oregano
Garlic frying in a beachside kantina
Skordalia and golden kalamari
A cold tin mug of pine-scented Retsina

* I blame MasterChef and that shouty gurning beachball on legs Gregg Wallace.

"My peas have not been arranged in the manner of the Arc de Triomphe. That's very disappointing".

"The menu said a drizzle of artisan truffle oil a la Turin Shroud. I can't see the face of Jesus on my plate at all!"

"Tonight Jocasta has made a seared loin of wildebeest in a lavender coulis with a ballotine of dodo in a foam of unicorn tears resting on a bed of pretension topped off by a tuille of privilege. This is fine dining now". This is utter bollocks sunshine.

HARRY POTTER & THE KITCHEN OF NIGHTMARES BY GORDON RAMSAY

(in which JK Rowling franchises out her Harry Potter series to other authors)

"You've got to be hard to bake souffles!" No you don't Gordon - put your pinny on and get back in the kitchen son.

"You fucking fuck you've fucked it
You fucking speccy twat!"
Said the machoman Michelin superstar chef
To the boy in the daft pointy hat

"Call yourself a fucking wizard?
You can't even conjure up toast!
You can stick your fucking broomstick right up your arse
You've just fucked my veal sweetbread pot roast!"

"Jesus H Christ in a sesame bun
Make me something that won't make me sick
If you fuck with my seared fucking woodcock
I'll sautee your bollocks you dick"

Young Potter bent over his cauldron
Stirring a stoat stroganoff
Et voila – his piece de resistance!
But Gordon looks fucking fucked off

"Fuck me Delia – what's this? Goblin goulash?
Who the fuck ordered that? Scooby Doo?
This is Claridges you fuck not the Merlin Motel
We don't serve fucking Halloween stew!"

So wee Harry he lay down his ladle
He twizzled his wand and he sang –
"Abrafuckingcadabra you fuckface!"
And Gordon Ramsay exploded. Fuck bang!

Had to perform this in front of school children once so substituted every swearie word with a parp on a bicycle horn. Was much funnier.

THE 7 EGGS OF MAN

Voice - Duchy Original e.g. if you want to say "yes" it should be pronounced "ears".

Breakfast

Decisions, decisions, decisions

Egg 1 – no – too runny
Egg 2 – no – too hard
Egg 3 – no – too cold
Egg 4 – no – the little soldiers are all burnt
Egg 5 – no – bloody awful, all squidgy – where's Delia when you need her?
Egg 6 – no – that's not organic, it's a Cadbury's Creme Egg!
Egg 7 – aargh! no! – looks like William Hague!

Camilla! Bring me a bacon roll!

Written for "Saturday Live" in 2006. It made my missus laugh. In his book "On Monarchy" Jeremy Paxman claimed that Prince Charles has seven boiled eggs cooked for his breakfast then lined up in ascending order of firmness, before only eating one. Chas has since refuted this allegation of culinary waste. To be fair to Paxo he did go on to say that that the story was so "preposterously extravagant as to be unbelievable".

The Countryside

A WINTER'S WALK IN WESSEX

On ground where Gabriel Oak once stood
Far from London's madding crowd
Trudging home through the mud of winter's dregs
Cross wind blasted heath, head bowed
Under Tess of the d'Urbervilles' gravestone sky
Stung by chill sea-salt rain, senses blunt
I survey the bleak grandeur and I realise why
Thomas Hardy was a miserable cunt*

* Maybe a wee bit harsh. Me, the missus and our dog moved to a godforsaken rural idyll in Dorset in 2002. The winters took a bit of getting used to.

AN ODE TO THE PACK OF MIDDLE-AGED MEN SHEATHED HEAD TO TOE IN THE UNSEEMLY BULGE OF FLUORESCENT LYCRA SHOUTING INANITIES AT EACH OTHER AT 7AM ON A SUNDAY MORNING WHILE THEY CAREER THROUGH MY VILLAGE SIX-A-BREAST LIKE SOME HIDEOUS, LIME-GREEN INSECT PESTILENCE ON WHEELS, HEADS DOWN, BONY ARSES IN THE AIR, OBLIVIOUS TO THE BEAUTIFUL SCENERY AND IN PARTICULAR TO THE TWAT FURIOUSLY GESTICULATING AT ME TO OVERTAKE HIM IN MY CAR ON A BLIND BEND BECAUSE HE THINKS THE ISLE OF PURBECK IS HIS OWN PRIVATE FUCKING VELODROME

That's the title. Here comes the poem. Bit of an anti-climax after that but let's press on.

You are not Chris Froome, you are not Chris Hoy
You are not Sir Bradley Wiggins
Your chances of winning the Tour de France
Are as fat as Christopher Biggins

I have a bicycle. I use it to collect a pizza. I do not wear ludicrous fancy dress to do so.

CHRISTMAS IN THE COUNTRY

Performed in a very poor, generic West country accent. Sort of Pam Ayres with laryngitis.

The snow was falling on the ground
"A Touch Of Frost" was on the telly
When the stranger came down our chimney
Red coat, white beard, fat belly

"Ho! Ho! Ho! I've got something for you!"
He laughed, in a manner quite coarse
And stinking of sherry he reached in his sack
So I shot him with reasonable force

CHRISTMAS IN THE COUNTRY NUMBER 2

'Tis the season to be jolly
A time of goodwill and great cheer
So you can tell that Joseph and Mary
We don't want no unmarried pregnant
   asylum seekers round here

CHRISTMAS IN THE COUNTRY NUMBER 3

'Allo, 'allo, 'allo?
Three well-whiskered wise guys with funny foreign names?
Bearing gifts suspiciously packed?
You're nicked for wearing tea towels and riding camels
Under the Prevention of Terrorism Act

> We discovered that they do things differently in the country. And we thought "Oh God, have we moved to Royston Vasey By The Sea?"

PURBECK – THE ENDURING ISLE

Cast adrift from city sirens, an island
A sculpture shaped from limestone, clay and shale
Flower's Barrow, Ballard Down, Old Harry Rocks –
Its steep backbone, the chalk spine of a whale

Brandy Bay, Tyneham Wood, land ploughed and drilled
Framed by wind-wracked cliff, shifting sand and heath
Crowned with a castle's shattered silhouette –
Albion's decayed, proudly ruined teeth

Veiled in ghostly sea-fog on wet dog days
Bathed in star-pav'd silent midnight skies
Where memories are cloaked in mason's dust
Flint-hard history seen through quarrymen's eyes

Whose muscle, grit and sweat built cathedrals
With the brittle chime of biddle and wedge
Cutting slabs from salt-sprayed, sepulchred caves
Tilly Whim, Winspit, Seacombe, Dancing Ledge

Thirst slaked clean by Square and Compass cider
As barrels clatter on the flagstone floor
Wood-panelled walls ingrained with song and story
Laughter echoing voices gone before

Mecca for apostles of the fossil
Trigonia and golden ammonite
The iguanodon's old coastal footpath
Two hundred million sun-cracked years bleached white

Angels slumber in the blue marble beds
With hammer on chisel they awaken
Iron-bound beauty slowly brought to light
Engraved deep in a past long forsaken

Now weekend cottages are haunted homes
And the gilded tourist shilling fills tills
Yet this is not England set in aspic
Still life draws breath from these ancient green hills

Timeless landscape for unhurried footsteps
A carving hewn from prehistoric bone
A deep seam of peace, space to think and dream
A living work of art, a precious stone

Written for BBC1's "The One Show".

On a previous appearance on this programme my tartan jacket clashed terribly with their hideous lime-green sofa

Purbeck is beautiful although it does become "Enduring the Isle of Purbeck" in the summer when the tourists arrive.

People have funny ideas about the English countryside. When the sun comes out beauty spots are invaded by the urban tastemaker second-home tourists "just down from London". All the Tristans and Isoldes in their Dolce & Gabbana weekend-tweed knickerbockers, turning the "Olde Village Shoppe" into their "rustic retreat", plastering it in Farrow & Ball donkey breath paint, making pomegranate chutney and having "country suppers" with Huge Furry Wetherspoon. And you realise that you can't "Escape to the Country".

The countryside is not as it's depicted in the brochures - it's not all flaxen-haired wenches, stout-hearted, ruddy-cheeked yeomen and a simple, homespun, bovine herd mentality. We don't all sit around the Aga with Kirstie Allsopp and a TV crew making a cradle from a walnut, knitting yurts from mouse droppings and icing cupcakes with the crystallised sweat of local peasants.

The countryside is misery, unemployment, alcoholism, jealousy, resentment, insecurity, bitter feuds, dead badgers, bigotry, mud, pigswill, chainsaw injuries, dubious dentistry, headless chickens, Fray Bentos steak 'n kidney pies and Arctic Roll from the Spar garage shop and the last flickering embers of a Wicker Man pyre round the back of the village hall on the night that the visiting Estonian mime troupe on the rural touring scheme went missing never to be seen again. But the views are good - so it's swings and roundabouts.

ARE YOU BEING SERVED?

You may be appalled to learn that poetry is not a lucrative career choice. Poets often have to supplement their income with other jobs to keep the wolf from the door. Sometimes they find the wolf on their sofa with his mates eating all the cheesy Wotsits and watching "Bargain Hunt". I got work as a barman in a gorgeous old anarchic pub. But the summer queues tested my patience and naturally sunny disposition.

Who's next? Anyone waiting? Can I help you?
Yes this is the bar. We have seventeen ciders.
Sparkling or still?
Would you like to try the home-pressed?
It's made here by the landlord.
Dry, medium or sweet?
Are you sure? The dry is very dry.
Dry like licking a blanket.
The menu?
Steak pasties, cheese 'n veg pie. Homemade.
No we don't do chips. Or sandwiches.
Two pints of Eve's Idea and two pasties
– £14.20 please. Cheers.
Cutlery and sauces in the next hatch.
Beers are on the blackboard in front of you.
In front of you.
Toilets are outside, turn left, on the left.
Yes – dogs are very welcome.
More so than some customers.
Dog bowl just there.
No – I'm afraid we don't take credit cards.
Cash only.
The nearest cash machine is Swanage.
Steak pasties and cheese 'n veg pie.
Ice and lemon? Half or a pint?
Do we have anything bitter yet hoppy?
There's a misanthropic rabbit round the back.
Pasties and pies. Pickled eggs.
No we don't do "children's meals".
Not even for little Tarquin.
The pub has been in the same family for over 100 years.
Salt 'n vinegar, cheese 'n onion, ready salted, Hula-Hoops, Mini-
    Cheddars, pork scratchings.
Cutlery and sauces are in the next hatch.
Sparkling or still cider? Dry, medium or sweet?
No, no Magners.

We have one red wine – it's a Chilean Pinot Noir.
Orange, grapefruit, pineapple, cranberry, tomato, bumbleberry, apple.
The toilets are outside on the left.
The building is about 300 years old.
No – we don't have wi-fi. Or a mobile signal.
Except from France.
We add everything up as we go along so if you can stick with the same person that would really help – we are not interchangeable serfs.
Yes the fossil museum is open.
No – that man is not an exhibit – that's Nobby. He's a regular.
The band is on about 9 o'clock.
The bus has gone I'm afraid. One a day. In August.
What's the medium cider like?
Medium. Causes flatulence.
You say "barman" I say beverage replenishment supply solution technician.
Taxi numbers are by the payphone in the corridor.
It's a phone you put your money in.
What do I recommend? I recommend you take some responsibility for your choice of drink – there's a queue stretching outside the door and down the hill and this rictus grin is merely masking the desolate despair gnawing at the very essence of my soul. Next!
The stuffed ginger badger in the tap room belonged to Thomas Hardy. He took it everywhere.
If little Tarquin could make his mind up about which sugary drink and snack he'd like we'd all be very grateful.
A please and a thank you would be nice Tarquin.
On the Atkins diet? Have a pickled egg and a vodka.
The toilets are straight down the hill – about two miles.
Do you really need another sambuca Derek?
Cutlery and sauces are on the roof and the jacuzzi is in the chicken shed.
Can I help you? Yes you sir. Sorry madam.
Stop chasing the chickens you wee shite!
I'm sorry I made little Tarquin cry.
I have Tourist Tourette's.
The wi-fi code is F.U.C.K.O.F.F Back to Fulham preferably.
Pomegranate 'n prickly pear, kumquat 'n coconut, lychee 'n lark's vomit
The pub is five years old.
It's a JD Wetherspoons flat-pack.
Roast unicorn 'n vinegar, smoky gnu, ostrich 'n onion.
That's your last sambuca Derek.

The sculpture is of Leon Trotsky.
He used to drink here in the 60's with Diana Dors and Basil Brush.
No we don't have toilets. We are but simple country folk. Yokels, bumpkins, teuchters. We're all related. Just piss anywhere outside. We all do.
No more sambuca Derek!
The pub is a figment of your fevered imagination and ten pints of Old Rosie. It does not exist.
Time gentlemen please.

It's a tough job being a poet, A lot of absinthe to drink., a lot of opium to smoke, a lot of reclining upon a velvet ottoman, thinking. Then there's the flouncing about on cliff-tops declaiming lovelorn verse in a fey manner. And sometimes you have to write as many as 17 syllables a day. That's seventeen! And you've got to condense a thousand ideas and complex feelings into those 17 syllables. Ain't easy.

VALEDICTORY HAIKU WRITTEN IN ANTICIPATION OF IAN BEALE'S EVENTUAL DEPARTURE ONE DAY PLEASE GOD FROM EASTENDERS*

Walford's codfather
Is sleeping with the fishes
Goodbye, Mr Chips

* First poem I ever performed. No idea if Ian Beale still owns a chippy. He might run a hipster coffee shop serving Phil Mitchell "artisanal brioches" for all I know.

SUDOKU HAIKU

5 syllables then
7 syllables and then
5 – oh no – fucked it

A HAIKU WRITTEN BY HERMAN VAN ROMPUY UPON BEING APPOINTED PRESIDENT OF THE EUROPEAN COUNCIL: "THE DEAD TREES OF FLEMISH WINTER BLOSSOM WITH NOVEMBER'S GOOD NEWS"

Up yours Tony Blair
Je suis le big cheese, not you
Take a running jump

BREAKING NEWS IN RURAL DORSET VILLAGE HAIKU

"Thatcher Dead" they said
Someone's fallen off a roof
I thought to myself

ENGLAND 1, TINY WEE ISLAND OF BJORK, COD, VOLCANOES, PUFFINS, 332,529 PEOPLE AND NOT ONE PROFESSIONAL FOOTBALL CLUB 2, HAIKU

Ha, ha, ha, ha, ha
Ha, ha, ha, ha, ha, ha, ha
Ha, ha, ha, ha, ha

Scotland may be shite at football but we're world class at schadenfreude. And we're allowed to be because we voted to remain in Europe.

BOOZE

CAVEAT COMPOTOR

This 2003 poem was published in that fine magazine "The Chap".

From eau de vie to usquebaugh
Via Chateauneuf-du-Pape
A snifter lets one's spirit soar
It fortifies a chap

A snort, a drop, a dram, a nip
Is what the doc prescribed
Unless the tincture gives you gyp
And should never be imbibed

So when mine host says it's your shout
Here's a whisper to the wise
There's a green moonshine one can do without
For that way madness lies

This wormwood grog scrubs out the brain
Fries talent to mirepoix
Many a Manet has gone down the drain
It sent Degas ga-ga

Chosen gargle of the aesthete
Its dangers – manifest
Toulouse-Lautrec shrunk by two feet
Van Gogh's left ear went west

It tastes of petrol and Polo Mints
It is a poisoned chalice
It makes this seasoned tippler wince
"Beware Absinthe of Malice"

ODE TO "THE SHUTTLECOCK 'N TURNIP"

Shall I compare thee to the Dog and Duck?
You are less shabby much more shabby chic
Watering hole of the braying young buck
Your DJ is chilled, your vibe so boutique
You scorn pickled eggs and pork scratching scrunch
"Have a sea-salt and balsamic cashew"
Pasties? Passé. Pin-striped ploughmen do brunch
"Braised rump of gnu in raspberry jus"
But cloth-capped ghosts drink at your zinc-topped bar
Their spit and sawdust memories no more
The snug was once their smoke-stained Shangri-La
Hounds sleeping on its fireside flagstone floor
Time gentlemen please to turn back the years
Let pubs be pubs again. Mine's a pint – cheers!

                    Look it's a bloody sonnet!
                        Well done me!

UISGE GU LEOIR

A siren sings in the Sound of Eriskay
Toss aside your cabers and barrel to the docks
Drown your sorrows in the Hebridean drink –
There's a shipful of Scotch on the rocks

Eau de vie, uisge beatha, water of life
Golden tears of the gods swept ashore
Soak up that "liquid sunshine", bathe in joy
Swim in whisky, whisky, whisky galore

Burns' John Barleycorn, king o' malted grain
A drop o' island rain and Highland peat
Taste the salty air, breathe in the angel's share
Sea-spray-smoky-honey-heather-sweet

Amber oil o' repartee dancing on the tongue
Whisky kisses burning on the lips
Bottled poetry in crates, ballads growled by Tom Waits
Give me a splash o' the sublime, a dram, a nip

Oh let me wade into a river o' Bruichladdich
Let me dive deep down in Edradour
Wash my sins away in Auchentoshan
Baptize me in a pool o' Aberlour

Aye – pour another whisky in my whisky
Just a wee deoch-an-doris, one more bar
And if anyone is listening up in Islay –
Mine's a ten year old Ardbeg* – slainte mhath!

* In 1941 the SS Politician sank just off a Scottish island with 28,000 cases of whisky on board. The story of the wreck was the basis for the book and film "Whisky Galore". In a shameless attempt to blag a free bottle of their fine nectar I hoped that someone at Ardbeg might be listening to this when it was broadcast on BBC Radio 4's "Saturday Live". Didn't work.

Quite happy to change it to Caol Ila or Laphroaig if anyone at those distilleries is reading. Or Glencadam. Or Edradour or any of the other brands mentioned. To be honest, any decent malt will do.

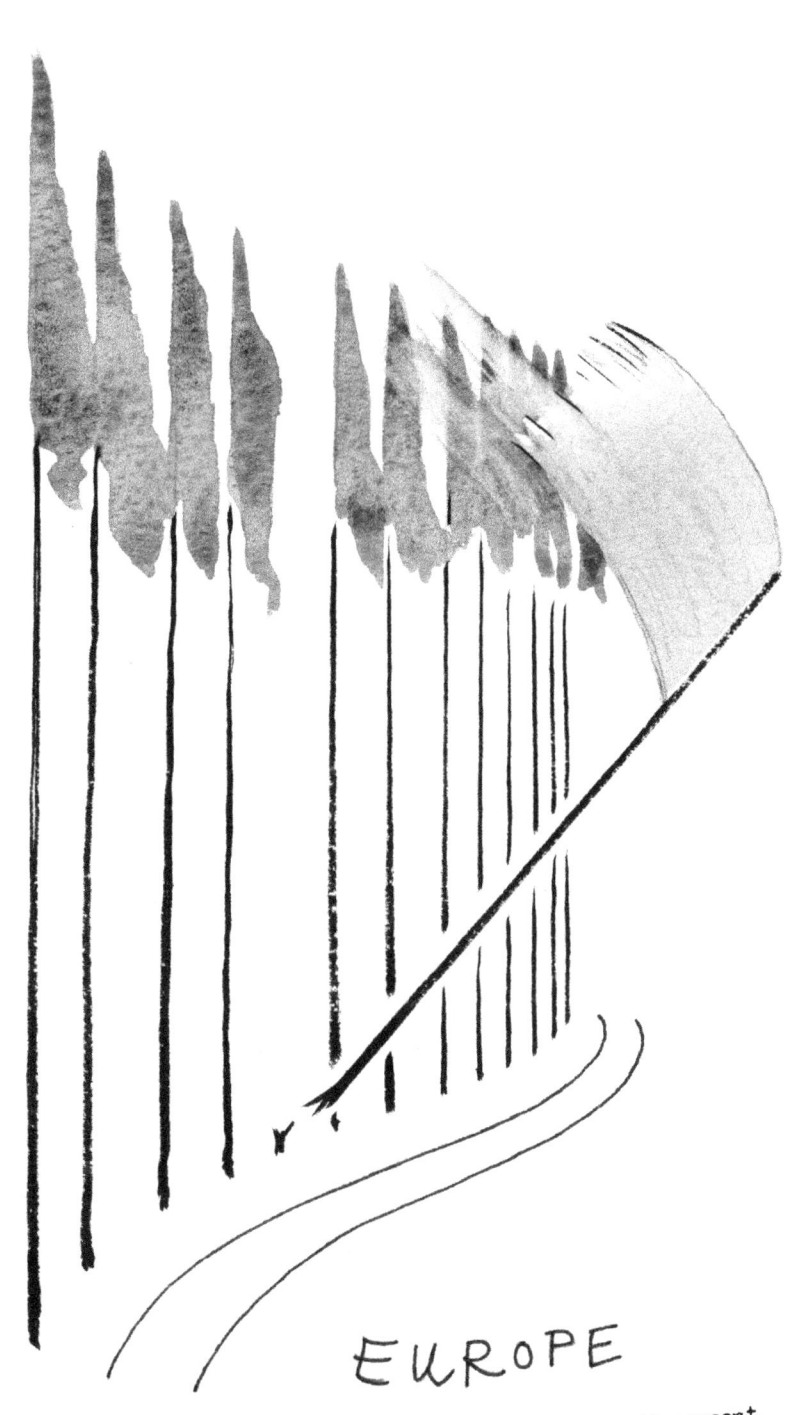

I WANNA DO THE CONTINENTAL*

It's time to carpe the diem con brio
Sing vive la difference amigo ooh la la
Ich kann nicht anders, que sera sera
I wanna whole lot of je ne sais quoi

I want to walk with the ghost of Paddy Fermor
Touch the Renaissance, breathe La Belle Epoque
Roam from Rotterdam to Constantinople
Bound for the Byzantine, Bauhaus and Baroque

I want to dally in a deli with Dali
Contemplate Kafka in a Krakow café
Share linguine with Fellini, frites with Magritte
Cycle backwards up the Champs-Elysees

I want to swim in a river of Rioja
Cross the Rhine's golden bridge with Charlemagne
I want to be Umberto Eco friendly
I want to build castles in Spain

I want to watch the subtitled "Lives of Others"
Sun-drenched Almodovar to bleak black nordic noir
Wear Sarah Lund's sweater while eating a bruschetta
"Troels! For helvede! Tak!" C'est wunderbar!

I want to be enraptured by Roby Lakatos
Manu Chao, Mozart, klezmer, cabarets
Drive a 2CV somewhere beyond the sea
Listen to Helen play a Chopin polonaise**

I want gypsy punk and immigrant funk
Give me Romany rock 'n roll
Electro-flamenco Balkan beats
Trip-hop-Mediterranean-soul

I want the Daily Mail to wail "he's foreign – send him back!"
I want to come over here and steal my own job
I want to wait tables, clean toilets, pick turnips, sweep streets
Just to irritate the bullet-headed Anglo-Saxon mob

I want to see the seamier side of Bohemia
Steep my soul in the velvety Aegean
Then give my weary bones a rest in the baths of Budapest***
Skal! Proost! Yamas! Je suis ein European

* Written in 2013 for "Saturday Live" before the word "Brexit" became fashionable.

** My missus can tinkle the ivories rather well.

*** I recommend the Gellert.

GREECE IS THE WORD

Olives up my nose, moussaka on my mind
Slathered in taramasalata
I'm Elvis El Greco of Greeceland
Don't care if I'm persona non grata

Ambrosia seeker, lotus eater
Eternally skint, Olympian debtor
I'm sailing up the creek with all the poor Greeks
Make mine a Metaxa, pass the feta

Gimme Aristotle and a bottle of Ouzo
Gimme sun, sea, sand and Socrates
The Venus de Milo floating on a lilo
Sweet honey on a little Plato please

Fountain of democracy, home of the Gods
A world of light, magical, magnetic
Where Homer means much more than Simpson
Land of classically proportioned aesthetics

Of Pythagoras, Pericles and Plutarch
Euripides, Achilles, Archimedes
Aristophanes, Sophocles and Sappho
Diomedes, Demis Roussos, Diabetes

Now it's Austerity for Mr Papadopoulos
Listen to the "Oxi! Oxi! Oxi!" Greek chorus
From corybantic excess to dystopian distress
This poem's written with the aid of a thesaurus

Elysium's whitewashed walls are graffitied
Between Scylla and Charybdis lies fear
Halcyon days are hazy memories
Here come Europa's purblind profiteers

Loan sharks peddling patronising myths
Handing down punishment that's Sisyphean
They're piling Pelion on top of Ossa
Time to leap into the deep blue Aegean

Go Hellenic – take a selfie at Delphi
Work the oracle and give Greece a chance
Raise a Retsina to Athena's wisdom
Bring out the bouzoukis and dance

Because figs cannot be gathered from thistles
Even Euclid couldn't square a bloody circle
EU-EC-ECB-IMF F-off
And take your beach towel off that lounger Mrs Merkel*

* I love Greece. I love its anarchy, it's generosity of spirit and it's very thick yoghourt. I hated watching the Troika's ghastly financiers privatising an entire country. Greece might as well have tried to raise cash from Duncan Bannatyne in his "Dragon's Den".

Then I thought - "oh God - does this mean I'm in bed with Nigel Farage, in a pair of striped pyjamas like Morecambe & Wise"? One look at Nigel's pompous, self-satisfied grin was enough to disabuse me of this notion. Wee Nigel is now the bellhop in Trump's golden elevator. "Ground floor lingerie, haberdashery, bigotry....going down....to eternal damnation".

And it seems that Angela Merkel is actually our best hope of stemming the "alt-right" tidal wave.

Our language is being debased. "Alt-right" just means Nazis in comfortable slacks doesn't it? "Post-truth" just means **bullshit.**

MAKING PLANS WITH NIGEL

I'm Spartacus! I'm Spartacus! I'm Spartacus-Alf-Garnett-us!
I'm a fearless freedom fighter – I smoke fags!
I'm Che Guevara in a Barbour jacket
My cocktail sausages have tiny purple yellow flags

A frothing pint of Olde Bigot landlord
A small sherry is the little lady's drink
Nudge, nudge, wink, wink, call a spade a spade
I'm not "racial" but I say what I think

The fuzzy-wuzzies don't like it up 'em
Chortle, chuckle, have another gin
The wretched refuse on our teeming shores
Is the white man's burden Gunga Din

Polish plumbers nicking British people's vowels
Romanian gypos stealing our kebabs
Lithuanians coming through our cat-flaps
Bulgarian lesbos driving minicabs

Fundamental Muslamist halal Wombles
Eating gay hummus and picking up our litter
Austrian transvestites growing British beards
Swedish detectives swigging Morse's bitter

Egyptian doctors, Nigerian nurses
Coming over here and saving lives
Bloody Bangladeshis cooking British baltis
Bloody politicians with their bloody German wives

Angela Merkin? Auf Wiedersehen pet
Ein Volk! Ein Reich! Ein Farage!
Liberte! Hostilite! Beyonce! Chardonnay!
Ooh la la Monsieur Nigel Fromage! *

* Lost the will to live at this point so the poem ends rather abruptly here.

HOW TO ASSEMBLE A SKALDESTYCKE*

Step one – check that Viking helmets are included
With vodka, saunas and a dragon tattoo
If any Volvo parts are missing – call Hans Blix
While Greta Garbo sings Abba's "Waterloo"

* Swedish for "poem"

Instal the existential angst of Kurt Wallander
(The pre-drilled Scandinavian detective)
Insert the dark, silent, frozen, gloomy winter
Hammer home the bleak and introspective

Attach a smorgasbord of Bjorn Borg and Bergman
To Anita Ekberg's Trevi Fountain frolic
Align the meatballs, tighten up the drunken elk
Adjust the tendency towards the melancholic

Reposition the fermented Baltic herring
Secure the Muppet Chef's flappen-jacken-ja
Nail down the Strindberg, discard the surplus Sven
Embellish with Ulrika-ka-ka-ka

Finally – paint it all bright blue and yellow
Finish with a super-sexy-blonde veneer
And that's a flat-pack poem made in Sweden
Without one cliched reference to Ikea

Written for BBC Radio 4's "Saturday Live". Sometimes inspiration doesn't strike. So thank goodness I was sat next to former weather presenter and "Shooting Stars" team captain Ulrika Jonsson so I had an excuse for this poem.

CARRY ON UP THE BREXIT*

"Look to your consciences and remember that the theatre of the world is wider than the realm of England" (Mary Queen of Scots, 1586).

Roll over Napoleon, sod-off Adolf Caesar
You're not grinning anymore Mona Lisa
Listen to the words of Mother Theresa **
Brexit means Brexit

* I voted Remain because I like Portuguese custard tarts.

Shoot yourself in the foot, throw dust in your eye
Jump off a cliff, plucky Englishmen can fly
Smack yourself in the face with a custard pie
Brexit means Brexit

Flat-pack furniture without instructions
A vacuum cleaner without any suction
Sherlock Holmes without deductions
Brexit means Brexit

Building sandcastles in the pissing rain
The people chose sandcastles – don't complain
Bucket, spade, anorak – soak up the pain
Brexit means Brexit

** Theresa May - she has the air of someone auditioning for the part of Death in an Ingmar Bergman film. Michael Gove on the other hand clearly spent over 20 years sat on the late ventriloquist Keith Harris's knee. "I wish I could run the country". "You can Michael, you can….oh, no, you can't….because you're a backstabbing wee numpty".

Pull up the drawbridge, fortify the shores
Turn back the clock, lock all the doors
Spotted dick, scurvy, saloon bar bores
Brexit means Brexit

Give two fingers to the liberal elite
Make the cosmopolitan obsolete
Ignore expertise, idiocracy's sweet
Brexit means Brexit

Repel the migrant armada, be prepared
Let their jungle burn, watch them running scared
Leave them all abandoned dans la merde
Brexshit means Brexshit

Jettison strangers, paddle your own canoe
Shout slitty-eyed abuse at Mr Wu
Send Paddington Bear back to darkest Peru
Brexit means Brexit

Replace the Pound with the Marmite Jar
Export Chelsea buns to Shangri-La
Sell Windsor Castle to Lady Gaga
Brexit means Brexit

Pay no heed to the hairy men in kilts
Be British, walk tall – like a corgi on stilts
Set fire to your continental quilts
Brexit means Brexit

Don't panic, keep calm, take control, Sieg Heil!
Don't mention the war, ha-ha, crack a smile
Laugh at Ed Balls dancing Gangnam Style
Brexit means Brexit

No openly gay Olympic fencing judges
No moaning metrosexuals bearing grudges
No benefit scroungers on cardboard crutches
Brexit means Brexit

Nul points Eurovision nobby-no-mates
Wave your pom-poms for Forrest Trump's Disunited States
Life's not a box of Belgian choc-o-lates
Brexit means Brexit

Feed your French croissant to the budgerigar
Stick a Danish pastry up your Nordic noir
Full English fry-up sir? Hip-hip-hoorah!
Breakfast means Breakfast

Walk upon these pastures green at last set free
Land of mighty leylandii and clotted cream tea
Sing Agadoo, push pineapple, shake the tree
Brexit means Brexit

Whack yourself round the head with a frying pan
Can you beat yourself senseless? Yes you can
More Viagra Nigel? That's a cunning plan
Hard Brexit means Hard Brexit

Claim Titanic success, drown in ticker tape
Get your trumpet out, play "The Great Escape"
Float off into the sunset, sinking ship shape
Brexit means We Are Fucked

ONE MAN'S MOUNT SINAI IS ANOTHER MAN'S PRIORY CLINIC

Forty days of fasting
Sparing, spartan, spent
If you're Charlie Sheen it's called rehab
For the rest of us it's Lent

EASTER

Christ crucified on Calvary is risen from the dead
Stigmata bathed in celestial light
And in the garden of Gethsemane a six-foot bunny's
Hidden chocolate eggs in the night *

* Easter is a confusing mix of crucifixion and confectionery. There's no mention of chocolate in the Bible. Or bunnies. Maybe only Jesus could see the Easter Bunny?

EAR SAY

Did Vincent Van Gogh chop his own ear off?
Was the lughole down the plughole his blow?
Or – on a starry, starry night did he get into a fight
Singin' – 'ere we Gaugin, 'ere we Gaugin, 'ere we go?

WORDY RAPPINGHOOD

It's time to bejewel the Queen's English
Like a sprachgefuhl Pygmalion
Will Self is in da house – respect
Let's get sesquipedalian

These four verses were written for BBC Radio 4's "Saturday Live" the last one whilst sat next to that excellent enemy of dull writing, Will Self.

PRIDE & PREJUDICE
by Jane Austen-Powers

Their eyes met across the vast ballroom
She felt her heart flutter awhile
As Mr Darcy, a man of much mystery
Approached with the hint of a smile

"I put the grrr into swinger baby!"
Said Mr Darcy to Elizabeth Bennet
Then with grave propriety he asked for her hand
"So let's swing baby – you're shagadelic!"

"You are too hasty, Sir!" cried Miss Bennet
"I must spurn your saucy advance
There are 300 pages to go in this book
Our romance is a slow, stately dance"

"Oh behave baby! You can't resist me!" said he
"Do I make you horny? I do!"
Just look at the size of my mojo
Yeah, groovy! Now let's boogaloo!"

"Sir, your comedy teeth are a cliche"
Said she, "Even for 1813,
Your Benny Hill banter is puerile
And your chest wig is frankly obscene"

"Yeah baby! So shall we shag now?" Darcy said
"Or shag later, after some drinks?
"You. Me. Handcuffs. Whipped cream
I bet you shag like a minx"

"Sir, I do not intend to 'shag' you" said she
"Not if you were the last man on earth
For it's a truth universally acknowledged
That I'm going to shag Colin Firth"

LADY CHATTERLEY'S LOVER
by DH Lawrence Llewelyn-Bowen

Lady Chatterley lived with Sir Clifford
In the wretched Wragby Hall
A dreary house of drab-brown stone
Whose décor had started to pall

Now m'lady was deeply frustrated
Her boudoir – a barren bad dream
She needed a love life makeover
So she called in the "Changing Rooms" team

"Oh! This bedroom is so geriatric!"*
"It's vile, it's baroque, it's rococo
Just look at the wallpaper – God what a yawn
The whole thing just screams night-time cocoa!"

*Said the dashing young designer – crushed velvet suit – frilly shirt – big cuffs – long, gorgeous hair.

"Darling, what you want is sassy, red-hot!
This is moribund, tragic, so tired!
Let's flounce down the path through the forest
Touch nature. Be bold. Get inspired!"

Off they skipped to the gamekeeper's cottage
(Wood-burning stove, shabby chic)
"It's earthy, it's virile, I love it!", he said
"The phallocentric motif is unique!"

"Let's make it a Gothic love palace
With a mock-rustic Pan-Asian vibe
In hunting pink Mexican tartan
Wow! That's a look I can barely describe!"

The front door swung open (MDF, tongue 'n groove)
As Mellors came home to his shed
"Oo's this ponce?" he said, strangling some pheasants
"And why's he painted me hut brothel red?"

The TV star purred, "It's your love shack"
Mellors growled, "It's nowt but cheap bourgeois veneer"
And whipping out his big Black 'n Decker
Nailed the fop to the shelf from Ikea

Mellors' manly machismo turned Lady C on
"Let's get dirty!" she cried "Clear the decks!"
So they hammered away and they screwed all night long
D-I-Y – it's the new British sex

DEAR HOUND

The late, great Miss Toots

Chocolate eyes
Marshmallow fur
Sticky paws
Sweet disposition
Sugar-plum wag
Fruity bark
She was Pavlova's dog

THE LILLIPUT CONSPIRACY

Can't help noticing that so many successful movie actors are quite short with big heads. I guess that must work on camera. But it must be difficult if you're Uma Thurman, Sigourney Weaver, Janet McTeer, Vanessa Redgrave, Billie Reynolds, Anjelica Huston, my wife etc.

Dustin Hoffman – Short arse

Tim Roth – Garden gnome

Robert De Niro – Not as big as you think

Tom Cruise – Bouncing weather dwarf

Sylvester Stallone – Surreptitious user of fruit boxes

James Dean – Fond of Cuban heels

Mel Gibson – Never read a porn mag because the top shelf is way too high

Liam Neeson – An exception that proves the rule

Danny DeVito – Res ipsa loquitur

Knock knock – Who's there?
Al Pacino – Al Pacino who?
Al Pacino who cannae reach the doorbell

Keanu Reeves – Average height but the acting ability of a flowerpot man

Ralph Fiennes – Uses a shoogly ladder to get into bed

The entire cast of "Lord Of The Rings" – Fucking elves

This town's too wee for most of us
The casting's all a fix
You'll never work in Hollywood
If you're over five foot six

TURKEY SHOOT

They deny it's a political decision
They insist it's a military request
They just need a few Scottish soldiers
To die at George Bush's behest

Doomed youth from Dundee and Dunfermline
Blairgowrie, Kirkcaldy and Perth
They've got you over a barrel of oil
In the Mesopotamian earth

You're a thin tartan line, off-kilter, laid bare
With a fig leaf of Downing Street lies
So that US Marines can break hearts and lose minds
In the name of MacFreedom 'n fries

Thus the red hackle rises west of Baghdad
The Black Watch have been here before
And the river Euphrates is foaming with blood
Now Babylon's burning once more

Star spangled rockets fracture the night
Minarets shatter and fall
The city of mosques* is a boneyard
Only ghosts heed the muezzin's call

"Allahu akbar! Allahu akbar! Allahu akbar!"
The cry from a death rattletrap
Hell-bent on a joyride to God with a bomb
Blasting metal and flesh into scrap

Charred carcass heaps high in the desert
Laid to waste for American greed
As democracy sinks in the quicksands of fear
And you smell the foul stench of this deed

But you're caught between the devil
And a sea of pitch-black gold
A sacrifice to the petrol pump price
Your honour is tarnished and sold

Still they say they'll disband your regiment
You're The Queen's Own Disposable Jocks
Then they promise you'll be home for Christmas
And you will – gift-wrapped in a six-foot pine box

* The Black Watch were sent to Camp Dogwood close to the "Triangle of Death" in 2004 to enable US Marines to flatten the city of Fallujah, "the city of mosques".

A JOLLY GOOD BUN-FIGHT*

When militant muslims misbehave
When they're hollering "Holy War!"
Sit them down with a nice hot brew
Because fighting them's oh such a bore

Don't let's be beastly to Jihad Joe
In his dreary Afghan grotto
Pick up a kettle, put down that gun
"Drop Scones – Not Bombs" that's our motto

So we're taking tea with the Taliban
Though they're terribly austere
They don't give a fig for Dundee cake
And they think Earl Grey is queer

Don't serve them Lapsang Souchong
Darjeeling or Typhoo
For they find it frightfully frivolous
To be asked "One lump or two?"

We're taking tea with the Taliban
And that Bin Laden chappy
When I said "Can I tempt you with a tart?"
He didn't look too happy

He feels that fondant fancies
Are fundamentally fey
Only infidels munch macaroons
Jammy Dodgers are risque

We're taking tea with the Taliban
But it's all going horribly wrong
One of them's caught his shalwar kameez
On my toasted-crumpet prong

They've flambeed the antimacassars
So the armchairs are now oily
And there's crumbs all over the Persian rug
Since they burnt Aunt Dolly's doily

We're taking tea with the Taliban
They're very Jalalabad boys
They've defenestrated the gramophone
Singing "Down with Satan's noise!"

* Written after marching against the Iraq War in 2003. "Make Tea Not War" placards were prominent. It did seem that the wrong people were in charge when "9/11" happened. We needed a more sophisticated response. If only Noel Coward had been running the country...

They're playing frisbee with the Wedgwood
It's Kabul in a china shop
They insist Aunt Dolly wear a burqa
She's in a filthy strop

We're taking tea with the Taliban
Aunt Dolly's boiling over
Patriarchal hegemony ain't her cuppa char
She's hit a mullah with a strawberry pavlova

The vicar's on the sherry
Aunt Dolly's off her trolley
She's serving up profiteroles
With a backhand smash and volley

We're taking tea with the Taliban
The dog is dribbling on Osama's djellaba
The vicar's put a tea towel on his head
Shouting "How's about that for Ali Baba?"

Aunt Dolly's gone Ramadan-a-ding-dong
Flinging flapjacks, slinging sugar-bowls
Fish paste finger sandwiches are flying through the air
With snacks 'n jugs 'n crockery 'n rolls

The Taliban are not amused
They're mujaheddin out the door
They say teapot diplomacy's right up the spout
They abhor chocolate Hobnob rapport

We're no longer taking tea with the Taliban
They're hiding in their cave in a huff
There's a trail of flaky pastry up the Khyber Pass
And beards full of clotted cream puff

But there's another nasty villain in the woodshed
Simply ghastly and exceedingly bad
He bakes lemon meringue pies of destruction
He's the moustachioed cad from Baghdad

He's a scoundrel, a bounder, a dangerous cove,
Loading up our currant buns ain't enough
He's planning Armageddon for a quarter past seven
By jingo! It's time to get tough!

So we're playing bingo with Saddam Hussein
All the four's – Shock and Awe – 44
We're off to a ballroom called Mecca
Eyes down for the Third World War

Bit of a tongue twister this one. Try performing it drunk at Glastonbury while being heckled by your wife.

OPERATION UNDYING CONFLICT

We're going to get the job done
We're giving it a final push
We're dropping bombs on goatherds
Up the Hindu Kush

We're exporting western values
We're making the streets of London safe and sound
We're importing heroin and body bags
We're driving fear and loathing underground

We're liberating the oppressed, we're defending democracy
We're installing freedom through force
We're neutralising the insurgents, we're pacifying targets
We're seeing it through, we're staying the course

We're only causing collateral damage
We're implementing extraordinary rendition
We're operating surgical strikes
We're accomplishing a just and stabilising mission

We're reconstructing a broken nation
We're building Jerusalem in Afghanistan
We're trampling through the blood-sodden poppy fields
With the ghost of Genghis Khan

We're in a struggle for civilisation
We're on a crusade against medieval vandals
We're tweaking Johnny Taliban's beard
We're stamping on his sandals

We're employing enhanced interrogation
We're imposing prolonged detention
We're pouring water down throats, we're punching heads
We're kicking the Geneva Convention

We're turning back the tide of terror
We're wearing King Canute's crown
We're trundling Sisyphus' rock to the top of the hill
We're watching it roll back down

We're chasing wild geese across the Khyber Pass
We're sifting dust in the Tora Bora
We're on the Silk Road to nowhere
We're opening a present from Pandora

We're harvesting death in a blighted land
We're staring into Pandemonium's cave
We're wrapped in the flag of faded hope and old glory
We're stumbling into Empire's grave

We're slowly sinking in the sand in a Soviet tank
We're unsheathing Darius of Persia's sword
We're putting new saddles on the same old donkeys
We're severing reason's golden cord

We're tying ourselves in a Gordian knot
We're weaving an endless wreath
We're climbing a mountain to catch a fish
We're seizing the moon by the teeth

We're ruffling a kangaroo's feathers, we're knitting with fog
We're nailing jelly to the walls
We're putting socks on an octopus, we're ploughing the sea
We're grabbing eunuchs by the balls

Alexander the Great, Blair, Brown, Disraeli
Cameron, Obama, Brezhnev, Bush
We're dropping bombs on goatherds
Up the Hindu Kush

Written in 2010 in the middle of the apparently endless "War on Terror" in Afghanistan.

NO REGRETS

Hand of history on his shoulder
The Lord Almighty's armchair soldier
Been there, done that, richer, older
Mr Blair has no regrets

Well-groomed, perfumed, well-heeled, well-fed
His "thoughts and prayers" with England's dead
Plastic poppies strewn upon his bed
Mr Blair has no regrets

No doubt, no qualms, no shame, no guilt
No crying over blood that's spilt
Team America to the hilt
Mr Blair has no regrets

Hidden weapons fairy story
Evil monster Jackanory
Sound the bugle of vainglory
Mr Blair has no regrets

Bad tyrants must be toppled over
What a lovely war Jehovah
Let's all sing "White Cliffs of Dover"
Mr Blair has no regrets

Non – il ne regrette rien monsieur
Combat's Edith Piaf bon viveur
Full metal jacket – suit you sir
Mr Blair has no regrets

Phosphorus burning in hell's forge
Uranium rising in the gorge
Cry God for Tony and St George
Mr Blair has no regrets

Walking wounded, widows on their knees
Screaming orphans, shell-shocked refugees
Slaughter, torture, butchered amputees
Mr Blair has no regrets

A hard rain falls like molten knives
On husbands, mothers, sons and wives
A thousand thousand wasted lives
Mr Blair says he regrets that bit

Eden turned to an endless Somme
Daily Baghdad bus queue bombs
Grim-visag'd peace, salaam, shalom
Mr Blair has no regrets

Cocooned in money for old rope
His soul whitewashed in holy soap
More infallible than the pope
Mr Blair has no regrets

He'll fight them on his tropical beach
In gung-ho after-dinner speech
On, on, once more unto the breach
Mr Blair has no regrets

Quite how Mr Tony could become Middle East peace envoy is baffling. It's like King Herod opening a Bethlehem kindergarten. It would have been more dignified if he'd gone on live telly dressed only in his underpants and played Lady Gaga's "Poker Face" on a kazoo.

The Weather

GLOBAL WARNING

Recycle, go green, save the planet
Don't burn holes in the sky
Stop the ice-caps melting
Or those wee Arctic Monkeys will die

That saves you watching Al Gore's film. Any eco-warriors feeling short-changed please read the Clarkson poem on page 44.

MOSTLY DREICH

Dark lours the tempest that howls overhead
A whirling dervish the wind twists and turns
Stars fall to earth as trees dropping fruit
A hurricane rumbles and churns

Jupiter readies his oak-cleaving bolts
Raising hell with dread rattling thunder
Whiplash lightning rips the celestial vault
As the heavens are rent asunder

Clouds of sackcloth cast a sullen shroud
Pregnant with pitiless pelting rain
The crumbling skies pour down their stinking pitch
In cacophonous desolate pain

Boreas' breath brings bleak, blasted blizzards
Freezing seas and Siberian doom
The land is plunged unto dank dismal depths
Of black, black Stygian gloom

Poseidon bursts forth on his mighty white horse
The shipwrecked shudder and cower in fear
And that's the end of the weather forecast
For the rest of the bloody year

THE WHITE STUFF

Winter's face is alabaster, bleak 'n blae
December wears a surly frown
A country lies silent in a frozen wreath
Benumbed and baffled the day is shut down

Blinding spindrift buffets the land
The bitter breath of Beira blasts forth
It is a snithing, sneaping, scouring wind
The air bites shrewd from the north

The skirling skies snitter full snart
Scowder turns to a soft, thick fleece
Flothers fall in sudden flurry
The old woman is plucking her geese

Niveous graupel sets like bone
The earth rings hard, a rutted trough
In brief – baby it's cold outside
A brass monkey's balls could drop off

But you can skite on the ice, toboggan round town
Slip-slide into a Breughel scene
Two fingers to pleurisy, frostbite 'n flu
Ski backwards down a glassy ravine

Dance with wolves and polar bears
Just go with the freezing flow
Cavort in the chaos of Albion's tundra
Let it snow, let it snow, let it snow

AUTUMNWATCH

Over a carpet of gold and burgundy leaves
In a pumpkin grin of flickering light
As russet apples fall into the cider press
Time's winged chariot stops in mid-flight

The sand in the hour-glass rises
The vampire is frozen mid-bite
Tock-tick, tock-tick, tock-tick, tock-tick
The clocks go back tonight

A GAME OF TWO HALVES *

Let's make poverty history
Let's be a force for good
Let's re-distribute all the wealth
Let's be like Robin Hood
Let's have no more paupers
Let's eradicate the rich
Let's empty out the bank account
Of Roman Abramovich

* An extended metaphor for a self-perpetuating oligarchy. Or a pointless rant. Whichever you prefer.

Let's syphon off his profits
Let's overthrow the petrol tsar
Let's give all his roubles back
To the workers of the USSR
Let's ask Jose Mourinho
"What's the Portuguese for poor?"
Let's cut his Amex card in two
Let him manage Stenhousemuir

Let's shove Sky TV where The Sun don't shine
Let Rupert Murdoch's empire fall
Let's reclaim the people's game
Let's get back our ball
Let's drop Ashley Cole down a deep dark hole
'Til he agrees that greed is wrong
Then we'll pay him 60 grand a week **
In Vietnamese dong

** Just 60 grand a week? That dates this poem. It was written over ten years ago.

Let's deport American owners
Singing "Soccer's going home!"
Let's bastardise their merchandise
Let's sell the Bobby Charlton comb
Let's raid Wayne Rooney's piggy bank
Let's put him in a fucking rage
Let's make him work with Gordon Fucking Ramsay
For the minimum fucking wage

Let's make Manchester City play on camels
In the sandstorms of Abu Dhabi
Let Ronaldo pay for his hair gel
By slaving as a cabby
Let's ransack Beckingham Palace
Let's give their bling to charity
Let's burn the mock Tudor mansions
Of football's aristocracy

Let's drive their Baby Bentleys
Over Beachy Head
Let's de-rail their gravy train
Let them take the bus instead
Let's ignore their tabloid sex romps
The Champagne Charlie songs
Let's dismiss their Double-D-list wives
In permatans and Prada thongs

Let the VIPs drink Bovril
Let their seats be cold and hard
Let's rip up their red carpet
Let's show them the red card
Let's wind up Football plc
Let's give the board P45's
Let's stop fat corporate bastards
Eating all the pies ***

Let's kick-off the revolution
Let have-nots have the final score
Let's hear "Manchester United nil
Partick Thistle four" ****
Let's invest Das Kapital
Let's end left-wing fatigue
Then poverty will be history
When there's a socialist premier league

*** I've started watching my new local team, Forest Green Rovers, the world's only vegan football club. The pies are quorn.

**** I should point out that I support St Johnstone not Partick Thistle but scansion required the latter.

BAD TIMES
(ARE JUST AROUND THE CORNER)*

The golden goose is stone cold dead
The party's over, the champagne is flat
Gordon Gekko's red braces have twanged in his face
The cream's curdled for cats who were fat

The whiff of despair hangs in the air
Farewell the sweet smell of excess
And it gets worse – by the end of this verse
Your house is worth ten per cent less

---

* In 2008 there was a "financial crisis". It turned out that the Emperor was in the bare, naked scuddy and the only banker in the country who knew what he was doing was the one on "Deal or No Deal".

Iceland banged up their bankers. We didn't. Ours still swagger round in their underpants of gilded ocelot, smoking cigars rolled on poverty's thigh and driving fur-lined Lamborghinis. Fair enough. No point in jailing bankers. We should have stormed the Gherkin and dragged them from their ivory tower then ritually disembowelled them with a plastic airline meal knife and left them in the desert to be picked to pieces very, very slowly by vultures on Mogadon while the "music" of Justin Bieber played at ear-bleeding volume on loop. Just for fun. Because the crash wasn't their fault.

It was all Kirstie Allsopp's fault. Her and Phil Thing (forgive him Lord he knows not what he does) with their bloody telly programme - "Hugo and Arabella would like to buy a weekend villa on the moon with enough bedrooms for all the horses and a city crash pad but they only have a budget of twifty billion" etc. Result - buy, sell, buy, sell, bada bing, bada boom and bust.

REPRIEVE

There's no justice in the hangman's rope
swinging in the air
There's no grace upon the gallows
there's no mercy in the chair
It's lynch mob yippee eye for an eye
string 'em up tooth for a tooth
Wild West values dressed in their Sunday best
vengeance burying the truth

But they won't hold the needle
they won't pull the switch
They won't buckle the leather straps
they'll just throw you in hell's ditch
Where Death is dressed in violent orange
and shackled to your fears
A silent, cold companion
as you wait and count the years

And though your hope seems broken
bruised and beaten black and blue
Don't drink the waters of oblivion
the world has not forgotten you
You will walk free from desolation
another life will come your way
And the blood-guilt stain on the Stars and Stripes
may be washed clean one day

Written for BBC Radio 4's "Saturday Live".

THE TWELFTH OF NEVER?

Pigs fly, fish climb trees
Snakes smoke cigarettes
Frogs grow beards, hens brush their teeth
Cows dance on ice in pirouettes

Bankers give their bonuses to nurses
Red snowflakes fall in freezing hell
Poets go on strike for a living wage
The country runs out of villanelles

Flowers bloom in bomb blasted Baghdad
Katie Hopkins has nothing to say
Donald Trump is locked up in Alcatraz *
And the key is thrown away

Celebrities no-one has heard of
Are left in the jungle to die
Gordon Ramsay eats himself
And nobody gives a fuck why

Jeremy Clarkson self combusts **
Rupert Murdoch hacks his own phone
Paris Hilton marries a trouser-press
Gorgons turn Piers Morgan to stone

The Taliban fly kites and drink whisky
Al-Qaeda dance their sandals off to funk
Tony Blair wears sackcloth and ashes
Gary Barlow becomes a Trappist monk

Eddie the Eagle flies like an angel
The next James Bond is Miles Jupp
Simon Cowell just melts like a witch
St Johnstone win the Scottish Cup ***

With backbone, pluck and cojones
Nerve of steel, heart of oak, iron chin
The hangdog Hancocks in homburg hats
All take on the world and win

Every underdog overcomes
The downtrodden rise up and sing
And the son of a Kenyan goatherd
Is crowned the new American King ****

* When this was written Mr Trump was a mere billionaire bully ruining the lives of the good folk living on the Menie Estate in Balmedie, Aberdeenshire with his golf course. Now he's President so he's unlikely to be locked up in Alcatraz. Let's lock him up in a minaret instead.

** Could substitute Philip Green here for Clarkson if you like. Not fussy.

*** On 17th May, 2014 St Johnstone beat Dundee Utd 2-0 to win the Scottish Cup. A glorious day. It actually happened. I was there - Row A, Seat 30, Jock Stein Lower Stand, Celtic Park.

**** Happy days back in 2008 when all was hope not grope.

LET THEM EAT FLAKE

Opal Fruits – not "Starbursts"! Treets – not "M&Ms"!
A Marathon is not a "Snickers Bar"!
Uncle Joe's Mintballs to "Krafty" Uncle Sam
Shut the lid on our nation's sweetie jar!

Yes a man's gotta chew what a man's gotta chew –
Highland Toffee, Jelly Babies, Twix
Now it's Crunchie time for every Fruit 'n Nut case –
Beware! Bounty hunters in our pick 'n mix!

Because a Finger of Fudge is just not enough
For the City boys' sticky fingered pillage
Singing Yankee Doodle dollar candy's dandy
Waving Stars 'n Stripes over Bourneville village

Chunky chocolate cowboys have shot the Milk Tray Man
Cup hands – there goes Cadburys way out west
Golden tickets go to boardroom Willy Wonkas
It's coming up Roses for the bankers who know best

They've got the Oompa-Loompas by the Curly Wurlys
It ain't no Picnic on the factory floor
The Billy Bunter fat cats get all the Creme Eggs
But if you work for Buttons – there's the door

So let's keep the family silver in the family
Scoff the last Rolo before it melts away
Let's Revel in proud Albion's confectionery
It's made British teeth what they are today

An iconic British brand was eaten up by a greedy American conglomerate. Don't let the corporate raiders get their cold, clammy hands on the NHS! Oops... looks like the sale has already started or what Jeremy Hunt calls "sustainability and transformation plans".

THAT GOVERNMENT HEALTHCARE POLICY IN FULL

Denigrate, degrade, defenestrate
Compassion's past its sell-by-date
Wave farewell to the Welfare State
Let the poor die

Demonise, deride, demoralise
Carve it all up, cut it down to size
Follow the profit, privatise
Let the poor die

Carry on doctor 24/7
All good nurses go to heaven
Don't need a new Aneurin Bevan
Just let the poor die

Alcopop-pizza-doughnut guts
Varicose veins, cigarette butts
Lousy lifestyle choices – tut, tut tut
Let the poor die

It's Charlie Darwin's natural selection
Healthy, wealthy Ubermenschen
Survival of the fittest pension
Let the poor die

Caring's simply too intensive
Pharmaceuticals – so expensive
Sign up for cover that's comprehensive
Let the poor die

No more needy "patients" in despair
You're valued customers of Virgin Care
Got no insurance? Say a little prayer
Let the poor die

Virgin Upper Class illness won't cost the earth
Choose Virgin syphilis, get your money's worth
Call the Virgin Midwife for a Virgin birth
Let the poor die

Three heart transplants for the price of two
Fast food surgery – drive on through
In an ambulance run by Deliveroo
Let the poor die

Pay for an Extra Special prognosis
The Finest drugs and diagnosis
Truly Irresistible tuberculosis
Let the poor die

Basic Saver service for the tightwad sod
Competitively priced, not too slipshod
Meet your consultant Mr Sweeney Todd
Let the poor die

Take an aspirin for your cancer
Call your local necromancer
Waiting room full? Here's the answer
Let the poor die

Depression is mere melancholy
Pull out that drip, get off that trolley
Beds are for clients with loadsa lolly
Let the poor die

Do something for nothing? Keep the receipt
Altruism is obsolete
NHS? New Harley Street
Let the poor die

Drown yourself in blood, sweat, tears and toil
Silently shuffle off this mortal coil
Shovelled six feet under Virgin soil
Let the poor die

Hey presto! No money! Disappearing trick
Dismantling our hospitals brick by brick
It's this government that's fucking sick
They'll just let the poor die

AN ANALYSIS OF THE EFFECTS UPON THE ARTS OF THE COLLAPSE OF AN UNFETTERED, FREE-MARKET, RISK-PRONE, PRIVATISING, PROFIT-DRIVEN, GREEDY-BASTARD, TURBO-CAPITALIST ECONOMIC SYSTEM AND THE CONCOMITANT ECONOMIC POLICY OF DEFICIT REDUCTION AND NEO-LIBERAL AUSTERITY MEASURES*

Times are hard
Belts are tight
Cupboards are empty
Pockets are light
Cuffs are frayed
Nerves are fraught
Cuts are deep **
Poems are short

* Some poor unfortunate child in Notting Hill must have been christened Austerity by now. "Austerity! Come in for your tea! Leave little Effluvia alone!"

** It turned out it wasn't hedge fund managers who'd brought the country to its knees but bloody benefit scroungers. So Bob Cratchit was put on a zero-hours contract and Tiny Tim had his disability benefits cut. And off to the food bank they went.

WHAT'S IN A NAME?

Morons, thugs and criminals
Copycat cretins, mindless mobs
Hoodlums, hooligans, Visigoths, vandals
Scurvy knaves, delinquent yobs

On a teenage rampage, running amok
Bovver boot boys for Beelzebub
Hell-bent on destruction of this country
Here they come – it's the Bullingdon Club

Apparel oft proclaims the man. If you wear a hoodie and help yourself to a pair of plimsolls from a burning shop in a riot that's called "looting". If you wear a £1,000 frock coat and trash a restaurant but Daddy foots the bill, that's "youthful indiscretion". Them's the sartorial vagaries.

QUESTION TIME

To be or not to be? That is the question
What does the fox say? That's another one
Who put the ram in the ramalamadingdong?
Where have all the good times gone?

How many roads must a chicken cross?
Are we human or are we dancer?
Is there life on Mars? Who ate all the pies?
Et tu Brute?* Is that your final answer?

Is this the real life? Is this just fantasy?
Where's Captain Kirk? Can you hear me Major Tom?
How do you hold a moonbeam in your hand?
Where do those lonely people all come from?

Is that all there is to the circus?
How many times does an angel fall?
Do androids dream of electric sheep?
Do they know it's Christmas time at all?

Where's the money Lebowski?
What ever happened to Baby Jane?
Would Jesus wear a Rolex?
What have they done to the rain?

Who's afraid of Virginia Wade?**
Shall I compare thee to a summer's day?
Is this your homework Larry?
Do you know the way to San Jose?

Who framed Roger Rabbit? Where's me jumper?
Can you hear the drums Fernando?
What time is love? How soon is now?
Tell me quando, quando, quando?

What's it all about Alfie?
What did you hear my blued eyed son?
And here's the 64 thousand dollar question
Oh America – what have you fucking done?

There's a cowboy builder in The White House
A racist golfer swinging to the right
An American idiot alchemist
Turning beauty into 18 holes of shite

A fat orange baby with a diamond rattle
An almighty dollar sign dead-eyed brute
Scowling-Oompa-Loompa-blowing-up-a-lilo face
Eric Cartman in a business suit

The Emperor of stark bollock naked lies
Putin's pet monkey grinding the organ***
A dime store B-movie Mafia boss
A personal friend of Piers Morgan****

A gold-plated fucktrumpet blaring out hate
Mr Dickchuckle-Fumblecunt unhinged clown
A shitgibbon screaming exclamation marks!
A tangerine cockwomble fouling Twitter Town

A hollow man, tiny finger on the button
"Nuclear holocaust. Bad. Very bad"
Will this be the way that the world ends?
Not with a bang but a tweet? (#sad!)

Where are we now? Where do we go from here?
Has the whole world gone crazy?
What's going on? You talkin' to me?
Parla usted Inglese?

What's so funny 'bout peace, love and understanding?
Wouldn't it be nice? Isn't that what makes a man?
When will there be a harvest for the world?
Can we fix it Bob the Builder? Yes we can

* Punning in Latin! You don't get that on "Live at the Apollo"!

** One of the finest refrains in pop music from Half Man Half Biscuit's "Outbreak of Vitas Gerulaitis".

*** Or is he? This line highlights the difficulties inherent in writing topical satirical verse.

**** They deserve each other.

NO MORE MR NICE GUY

Gonna smear myself in aspiration
The gravy train is in the station
El Dorado is my destination
No more Mr Nice Guy

Goodbye caravan park in Dundee
Hello bloated banker bourgeoisie
I'm Business Poet plc
No more Mr Nice Guy

Outsource my sonnets, commodify
Churn out cheap dross and pile it high
Do more advertisements than Stephen Fry
No more Mr Nice Guy

Flex my corporate muscle, do the hustle
Dance through tax loopholes like Darcey Bussell*
Become a brand – and I don't mean Russell
No more Mr Nice Guy

Go global, franchise out my doggerel
Elvis Multinational McGonagall
Use any shite rhyme that's vaguely probable
No more Mr Nice Guy

Import sweatshop haikus factory fresh
Seventeen syllables made in Bangladesh
Work 'em to the bone, get my pound of flesh
No more Mr Nice Guy

Feel no guilt – my profit's private
Wash my hands like Pontius Pilate
Sell my granny to Somali pirates
No more Mr Nice Guy

Fuck the morals – they don't matter
Move the goalposts, bend it like Blatter
Milk the system and fry it in batter
No more Mr Nice Guy

King of bling, tangerine-tanned lump
Kick sand in your face, bamboozle, gazump
Iambic pentameter's Donald Trump**
No more Mr Nice Guy

Solid gold sporran, Gucci gear
Look at the size of my chandelier
On first name terms with Vladimir
No more Mr Nice Guy

Scribble Satan's verse, the Devil's villanelle
Shrivelled walnut soul in an empty shell
For Christ's sake shoot me – I'll see you all in hell
No more Mr Nice Guy

* I mean dance like Darcey Bussell not that she avoids tax.

** "My whole life is about winning" (D.Trump) British culture has become all-American winner takes it all, win, win, win at all costs. It's all Team GB and gold medals for synchronised-equestrian-ping-pong and clay-pigeon-canoe-ball. Even baking a bloody cake has become a competition. You can't just bake your cake and eat it. Oh no. Your fondant fancies must be judged by the improbably named Paul Hollywood and his equally improbable beard. And if they're not good enough then get outside and shoot yourself.

I blame Professor Frederick Mercury of Queen's College who asserted that "We are the champions - no time for losers".

I preferred the heroic floundering of Eddie the Eagle. Or Nigel Havers in a tweed vest, Brylcreemed hair, plimsolls, pipe, champagne flute in hand finishing last in the egg and spoon race.

Nigel would get short shrift now - "You lost. Why? You've let yourself down. You've let your family down. You've let your friends down. You've let the country down. How do you feel? Do you feel small? Do you feel worthless? Do you feel suicidal? Will you kill yourself? Now? On live telly? At least cry! It's an emotional journey!"

But maybe I could be a winner. Relax in my exclusive-elite-lifestyle-facility-apartment sipping a cappuccino with my frosted trophy wife and Midwich Cuckoo children whilst wearing an individually monogrammed dressing gown like I imagine Roger Federer might do on a Sunday morning, smiling smugly but ever so humbly at my good fortune to be living the dream. No time for losers. Just got to get with the zeitgeist.

IF....WITH APOLOGIES TO KIPLING (RUDYARD NOT MR)

If you can keep your daddy's dollars free from tax
If you can grope women and put them in their place
If you can tweet the world alternative facts
If you can kick sand in every Muslim's face
If you can have a "great relationship" with "*the* blacks"
If you can wear your arrogance like cheap cologne
If you can feed your empty soul with golden Big Macs
If you can blow your own tiny trombone
If you can contradict yourself inside a minute
If you know you've bought the race before it's run
Yours is America and all the fear in it
And – which is more – you'll be the President my son

Fear is the currency that "politicians" like Trump and Farage trade in.

In July 2015 a British tabloid ran the headline "Migrants Ruin Big Holiday Getaway". Those thoughtless, loser migrants eh? Escaping wars we started, torture, famine, genocide, poverty, disease. Walking through deserts, sailing leaky dinghies across the Med, hanging off lorries in Calais, breaking the world record for 31.4 miles running through the Channel Tunnel while poor British tourists are stuck in a traffic jam when they should be sipping a nice chilled Chardonnay in a flowery meadow in Provence. Selfish bastard migrants.

There's a refugee crisis in Europe but Nigel Farage is on top of the White Cliffs of Dover shouting "No room!" like the Mad Hatter at his tea party.

Sometimes I despair of the human race. We're just over-evolved chimpanzees with the manual dexterity to zip up our onesies.

And when did romper suits become "onesies" eh? Did I miss a meeting? "Ooh look at me, I'm going to tweet a selfie of me in my onesie, smiley face, smiley face, smiley face, thumbs up, LOL!" Use fucking words! We're going backwards.

No wonder you can't make a living doing poetry. Fuck the poetry. Tribute bands that's the way forward. Never out of work. So I'm looking for four similarly knackered, dishevelled, middle-aged men and we are going to form "Onesie Direction". We'll clean up.

WALLS *

From Jericho to Jerusalem
From the Solway Firth to the River Tyne
Walls fortify, defend, secure
Walls draw the battle line

Walls brick up understanding
Walls exercise control
Walls are silent, walls have ears
Walls exact their toll

Walls entomb, walls divide
Walls barricade the unknown
Berlin, Belfast, Gaza, Mexico **
Walls set difference in stone

But the same sun that sets on the West Bank
Rises up on the eastern wall
A man's a man in Mesopotomia
A man's a man in Gaul

Forget all creeds, forget all colours
Pay no heed to flag or crown
Then one day we may live in peace
When the walls come tumbling down

* This was an insert written for Julie Matthews' song "Rock of Gelt" in 2010's "All Along The Wall" project.

** Mexican wall not built at time of publication but pending.

Walls also make sausages and ice-cream. Other brands are available.

RISE UP

Dedicated to the memory of Jo Cox

This scepter'd isle is now a nation of landlords
This realm's a retail park for oligarch and sheikh
Waterloo sunset has been sold for a crock of gold
We've been pimped out to pin-striped bastards on the make

The banker's got the whole world in his wallet
The robber baron blusters in his boardroom chair
The squire rules at will from his mansion on the hill
The politician is a multi-millionaire

Come all you Diggers, you Ranters, you rebels
Shout from the rooftops, make your voices heard
Come all you artists, you thinkers, you dreamers
Share your vision, unbowed and undeterred

Come all you tempest tossed poor huddled masses
You sick and tired, you overworked and underpaid
Come all you burger flippers and baristas
You nurses, teachers, carers, chambermaids

Rise up like Shelley's lions after slumber
Leave your mind-forg'd manacles behind
Rise up together and reclaim this other Eden
Rise up and have the courage to be kind

GLASTO

In the mythical Vale of Avalon
Beneath the teardrop of Glastonbury Tor
Where Joseph of Arimathea once walked
By the hallowed hawthorn of yore

On the burial ground of the Holy Grail
Where King Arthur's soul was set free
A rockabilly vicar in a tutu
Plays a didgeridoo up a tree

It's a wild Wild West shanty town
It's the Pilton village fete
It's the Lord Mayor of Misrule's annual show
It's a bucolic mini-state

It's beards 'n bongos, beads 'n bells
It's a farmer of karma 'n kagoules
It's fields bathed in fairy dust
It's a Babylon of holy fools

It's the BoHo House at Worthy Farm
Where peace and love are the crop
It's a trip through the canyons of Dali's mind
On a leyline to the pyramid of pop

It's proud Albion's Billy Braggstock
It's John Peel's Somerset Shangri-La
It's a sou'wester fiesta
It's the Millets Mardi Gras

It's anarchy in a Cath Kidston yurt
It's a Mad Hatter's silent rave
It's eco-friendly-fairtrade drum 'n bass
It's techo-techno Chas 'n Dave

It's an explosion in Willy Wonka's factory
It's a caramel chocolate swamp
It's a barmy army's welly boot camp
It's a shock troop's rock 'n roll yomp

It's the psychedelic cider solstice
It's the Battle of the Portaloo,
It's the people's pleasure garden
It's inhibition's Waterloo

It's seventh heaven up on cloud nine
It's a human zoo, the eighth deadly sin
It's a mystical, magical merry-go-round
It's "Glasto!" – it does what it says on the tin

Written as Glastonbury's official poet-in-residence in 2007.

BRISTOL – A RECIPE*

Take one place way out in the mild, mild west
Light the Gas, get out a melting pot
Throw in merchants, Methodists and pirates
Mix Georgian splendour with graffitied squat

Marinade slowly in rum and sugar
Smoke in hand-rolled tobacco by the docks
Sear its past with the scars of slavery
Infuse its soul with the unorthodox

Whisk up a bridge across the Avon Gorge
Steam in the shipshape fashion of Brunel
Blend Wallace and Gromit's cracking ideas
With Concorde's supersonic farewell

Beat drum 'n bass 'n dub into trip-hop
Wallop in a dollop of Banksy's wit
Preserve pride in a People's Republic
Flambé in a riot of colour and grit

Melt Fry's chocolate, stir in Nathan Filer's words
Add Chris and Johnny Morris – a pinch of each
Pour in a blue glass of rich Harvey's Cream
Sprinkle with the stardust of Archibald Leach

Season and spice with DJ Derek's reggae
Braise in cider and anarchic spirit
Drizzle in "Brizzle" a la Julie Burchill
"Awright me old babber, mazen', innit?"

Garnish with the Old Vic's "Salad Days"
Serve chilled out and downtempo, don't rush
A radical dish, full of flavours, yer tiz –
Just a little taste of Bristol – gert lush

> * Written for "Saturday Live" at the Bristol Food Connections festival in 2014. Should really have a reference to Burning Eye Books in this poem. Apologies Clive and Jenn.

FROTHING MAD

Wake up and smell the profit
It's a roasted bean bonanza
They've struck it rich with hot black gold
It's a cost-a-packet coffee shop extravaganza

It's flat-pack counterculture
High-street wi-fi boho beige
But I'm the Don Quixote of the daily grind
On the boil with Java rage

No. I don't "wanna blueberry muffin with that?"
Or a "funky blend from Guadalajara"
Hey Mister Barista, I'm no mug
I'm caffeine's Che Guevara

Fighting the blight of the tall-skinny-latte
Caramel-decaff-cappuccino
Double-chocca-mocha-macchiato
Wet-whipless-triple-frappuccino

Shot-in-the-dark-with-a-hazelnut
Long-black-flat-white-with-wings
And those polythene-cheesy-panini
Burn-your-mouth-off-toastie-things

Why don't they charge for Small, Medium, Large?
Why's it Primo-Vente-Grande
Mucho-Macho-Ridiculoso
Massivo-Pavarotti-Elephante?

Yes, I stand alone like King Canute
Against the relentless corporate tide
Of the "have-a-nice-day" megabucks café
The bland leading the bland worldwide

It's all that Jennifer Aniston's fault
Her and her "Friends" at "Central Perk"
Sipping "no-fun-drip-with-soya"
Driving me berserk

So head held high I head back home
Past the old greasy spoon, RIP
To lead the revolution from my armchair
Feet up with a nice cup of tea*

* Like "Twin Peaks'" special agent Dale Cooper I appreciate "a damn fine cup of coffee". This was written for "Saturday Live" about a listener who hated the British High Street becoming completely Starbuck-ed.

Now we have "artisan" coffee shops called things like "Cake & Danger" or "Spoon & Cupboard" full of bearded, tattooed young men who look like Edwardian taxidermists, hipster baristas in flat caps, jeggings and no socks serving up "a shot of Java, nix on the moo juice". Christ I feel old.

* I tried

* I tried

Grand Royal Finale

The Queen may appear to be a slightly grumpy dinner lady in a P Diddy hat but beneath her mysterious Sphinx like exterior there lies a seething mass of emotions.

I know for a fact that her preferred genre of music is gangsta rap. Check out her millinery - that's the clue. Which explains why she looks bored rigid on state occasions when they wheel out the likes of Lord Gary of Barlow for her "entertainment". She hates that stuff.

Shouldn't be any surprise because gangsta rap and the monarchy have similar levels of pomp and circumstance. Anyway, this next poem is what she really wants to say when they give her a speech to read. She can bust a rhyme that girl.

THE QUEEN'S SPEECH
Voice – sort of posh Widow Twankey.

My government will meet the aspirations of the nation
Introducing legislation to promote regeneration

Who writes this stuff? It's so mundane
It's my speech – let's start again

Word up you commoners, serfs and tramps
I'm that woman from awf of the stamps

Yo! Rule, Britannia! Sing hosanna!
Don't anybody dare mention Diana

I'm the pearly queen, I'm England's rose
You's my bitches, you's my ho's

Castles, palaces, livin' it large
Diamond-studded golden barge

21st century Cleopatra
Bessie in da big house comin' at ya

Floating up the Thames in me royal flotilla
Why's that horse in a hat? Oh no – it's Camilla

Curtsy, bow, kowtow, grovel
Fly a little flag from your ghastly hovel

Flap those tea towels, swing from the bunting
Pour me a gin – let's go hunting

We're the Windsor posse one cannot quarrel
Shoot some peasants at Balmoral

(Terribly sorry that should be "pheasants"
not "peasants" – Freudian slip)

I got the guns, I got the bling
The Prince of Biscuits will never be king

Prince Will.i.am is the family mascot
Hats on homies big it up at Ascot

Fo shizzle my nizzle – pardon one's French
We diss Helen Mirren and Judi Dench

I'm Her Majesty – they're absurd
Give me an Oscar – I'm James Bond's bird

Cut some ribbons, shake some hands
Sit through another boring military band

Wave, wave, wave, wave, wave
Wave, wave, wave, wave, wave

Oh Christ! Cliff Richard! Pass the paracetamol
Bring on the dancing corgis – so much better LOL

And don't complain about the language –
It's my fucking English – have another sandwich

Build me a yacht, roast me a swan
Bring me the head of bloody Elton John

Behold my crown – see it dazzle
Prince Harry says Andrew's a bit of a vajazzle

Get down with the youth, ignore all syntax
Like, y'know, whatever, hashtag chillax

Headscarf, tweeds and a sensible brogue
Don't just stand there Philip – c'mon vogue!

Cheer up Brexit Britain, let's have another jubilee
God won't help you – he's busy saving me *

* That's my OBE gone.

.

THE END

That's all folks!

Night, night.

Take the needle off the record.

THANKS AND ACKNOWLEDGEMENTS

Thanks to Clive Birnie and Jenn Hart at Burning Eye Books.

To Luke Wright and the Nasty Little Press posse.

To Frank Stirling at Unique and everyone involved in "Elvis McGonagall Takes A Look On The Bright Side".

To all the lovely folk who sponsored my 2015 Edinburgh show "Countrybile" (the Laura Kinsella Foundation, Kit & Val Braunholtz, Katy Fisher, Arthur Gordon, Jeremy Grant, Peter & Deborah Handy, Bryan & Tracey Leitch, Barbara McGeary, Marcus Moore, Joan Moynihan, Marion & Bella Norman, Andy Parsons (not the baldy one), Sue Perkins, Naomi & Jeff Vanderwolk, Glynn Webster and Andy Wells).

To all my mates on the stand-up poetry circuit and all the tireless promoters who've booked me for gigs.

To Tony Kerins for the illustrations.

To Anna McCarthy for the cover photo.

To Adrian Mealing at UK Touring.

To Matthew Crampton at the Crampton Motel.

To Rob Ogden at Ogden & Brown, Dodecanese Tour Management.

And to Helen for inspiration and more support than I could ever expect or possibly deserve.

A number of poems in this book were published by Nasty Little Press in "Mostly Dreich" and some were commissioned by various TV and radio programmes where indicated.

www.ingramcontent.com/pod-product-compliance
Ingram Content Group UK Ltd.
Pitfield, Milton Keynes, MK11 3LW, UK
UKHW031001260625
460105UK00002B/111